CATCH THE WIND

August 11, 2005

Adrian,

Of all my friends, I think you and I have shared the most adventures together! Whether it was breakin' in Calgary, Stony Plain's First (and only) rave, or the Real Deal, you and I have stuck it out together. I hope we have many more!

Thanks for your commitment to the shop. My prayer is that it will thrive and that we can use the business to bless others.

You know I'm excited about this book. I hope you read it and get excited too!

Your friend,
Justin

PS: Happy Birthday!

CATCH THE WIND

THE SHAPE OF THE CHURCH TO COME
—AND OUR PLACE IN IT

CHARLES RINGMA

REGENT COLLEGE PUBLISHING
Vancouver, British Columbia

This edition published 2003 by
Regent College Publishing
5800 University Boulevard
Vancouver, British Columbia
V6T 2E4 Canada
www.regentpublishing.com

Views and opinions expressed in works published by Regent College Publishing are those of the author(s) and may not necessarily represent the official position of Regent College <www.regent-college.edu>.

National Library of Canada Cataloguing in Publication Data

Ringma, Charles R.
    Catch the Wind

    Includes bibliographical references
    ISBN 1-57383-266-9

    1. Mission of the church. I. Title.

BV601.8.R56 2003   262'.7   C00-911377-0

CONTENTS

PREFACE

This book on the church has come first and foremost out of long and painful struggle rather than mere academic concerns. What made the struggle particularly difficult was two seemingly unresolvable tensions. The first was the tension between my experience of both the institutional church and my involvement in alternative Christian community. Instead of settling for the one in preference to the other, I believed that both forms of being church needed to be interacting creatively.

The second was the tension between church—whether institu-tional or community-based—and world. Since the church does not simply exist for itself, it has to be relevant to the world. In believing this I was constantly torn between being faithful to the church and relevant to the marketplace.

Whether the marketplace was the city's darkened streets with its alienated young people, or the public service, or private industry, or the hallowed halls of academia, the response has hardly been different. People were fascinated by Jesus, but at worst they despised the church and at best thought it was largely irrelevant.

For some years I naively thought that this was not a major problem. "Give people time to understand Jesus' words and they will come to terms with being part of the church," I thought. This certainty began to be shaken. Not only did people fail to make the crossover from Jesus to church, but people in the church were making their way out the back door.

What was common to both those in the church and those outside it was that the complexity of the church was too far removed from the simplicity of the Gospels and that the organisational machinery of the church undermined the radical freedom in Christ articulated in the Epistles. In other words, they identified a big gap between Jesus' vision of life and that of institutional Christianity.

I found all this particularly troublesome. It was amazing to see drug addicts and prostitutes embrace a new life in Christ. But it was appalling to see their difficulties in becoming socialised into the life of the church. The church was more a uniform culture than a diverse community of disciples.

All of this was further complicated by the fact that so much of the sharing, serving, praying and caring that occurred informally in the marketplace and in our homes seemed to exhibit what church should be about. In other words, the less we formally tried to be church, the more we were able to link up with people and enter their issues and struggles.

This occurred particularly in the practice of hospitality in our homes. People came to faith in Christ and developed commitments and discipleship not because they were formally evangelised or ministered to. This took place instead in the midst of friendship building, sharing life together and involvement in the common duties of cooking, house cleaning, fun nights, talking and opening our lives to one another.

This kind of lifestyle had the mark of reality and the ring of authenticity. Church, on the other hand, seemed formal or inauthentic. It seemed too removed from ordinary life. Here life was shared, while in the Sunday experience of church, certain religious ceremonies predominated.

This book attempts to resolve some of these tensions. It is based on the premise that being church can be different. It recognises that God's idea of church is good, but that we are responsible for the human face of the church. We create its forms and structures. We make the rules.

What we have created has been less than helpful. Church has not joined people together in empowering ways and it has failed to build meaningful bridges into our secular world. Instead, we have built churches that are either so "holy" that they are world-denying or so pragmatic that they have no transforming power. But the problem common to both groups is that the theological agendas of the leadership and organisational realities of the institution predominate rather than the concerns and issues of the people who comprise the church.

In other words, the people of God are frequently peripheral in the very institution that claims to serve them.

I believe that it is time to change the rules. For a long time the church in the West has not done well. It has found itself on the sidelines as an ineffective moral guardian. Under the guise of maintaining a biblical ethic, it has often promoted an outmoded mentality. It has clung to an old world of permanence and certainty that has been fast slipping away.

As a result, the church has hardly been formative in shaping the larger issues of the modern world. While it has faithfully trained men (and now women) for ministry in the church, it has not sufficiently trained them for their task in the world. Church building rather than kingdom building has been the focus. As a consequence, the Christian contribution to the sciences, the arts and politics has been less than what it could be.

9

Moreover, the church's own life has not been characterised by genuine community and a costly discipleship that has identified it with the cry of the poor and the oppressed. As a largely conservative, middle-class phenomenon, the church in the West has not been able to re-establish its links with the working class and finds it difficult to incorporate into its life the marginalised in our society. It is no longer the champion of the poor as it was in the days of Wesley.

Fortunately, the church in the developing world has done better and acts as a signpost that things can be done differently in our part of the world. In its base ecclesial communities, the church in the Third World has demonstrated the power of the church of the poor. Here spirituality meets social justice and the church community opens its arms to its poor and needy neighbours.

This is not to suggest that the church in the developing world is trouble-free and the church in the West is full of difficulties. This kind of simplicity must be resisted. But the church in the West needs a renewal that moves well beyond the charismatic renewal of the last decades. Renewed people in old structures ultimately fail to gain a forward momentum.

The focus of this book, however, is not to propose a blueprint for new structures, but to concentrate on helpful *processes* that empower people for community and justice.

In attempting to sketch how church may be different, I am not expecting to win a lot of support. Some theologians won't appreciate this work because its pages are not peppered with the big names in theology—Barth, Bultmann, Pannenberg, Rahner and Moltmann. This has been done deliberately and has nothing to do with a lack of familiarity with or appreciation of their theological positions. Rather, the focus of this book is not so much to engender discussion limited to academics as to engage the general reader.

Some clergy might not like this approach because it threatens their power base. Some denominational leaders may well label it sectarian. Many conservatives will reject it because it doesn't fit their particular interpretation of Scripture. But I beg their careful reading. This book essentially is not iconoclastic. While it is critical of current structures, it contains a vision of a renewed church.

My primary target audience, however, are two groups of people. The first are those who have tirelessly worked for change in the institutional church and have given up. They have become stranded. They have no energy to try again and no motivation to attempt to create something outside of the traditional church structures. I have met many such fine people. Battered by the battle, they are marooned.

The second group are the valiant few who have attempted alternative ways of being church. These are the people who have formed intentional Christian communities or house churches, but have found over time that they are walking a lonely road and consequently have become more inward focussed.

My appeal to both these groups is to go *further* with change in order to empower people.

I have also a third, fourth and fifth group of people in view. The third group are those who have severed links with the church. They are still women and men of faith, prayer and service, but they have become alienated. I have many people in mind in this category, but one story will suffice. This family maintains family prayers and spends time reflecting on Scripture. The husband has brought a carefully thought-out set of values to the workplace, making him an exemplary Christian. The mother is a woman of deep prayer and the children have a keen Christian witness at school. But they hardly ever darken a church door. I trust that for people such as these this book will encourage them to join with others in the journey of faith.

The fourth group are those who are deeply dissatisfied with the church but remain immobilised. These people have neither worked for change within the church nor have they attempted alternatives. They are simply unhappy with the way things are. Their immobility may be due to many and varied factors, but frequently the most basic is that they are still operating with the old model of church where spiritual goods and services are expected to be provided for them. While they are unhappy with these services, they have little sense that *they* are the church and that they have a responsibility for their own development.

I hope for them this book will be a catalyst for action as they grasp a new sense of responsibility.

The fifth group this book has in view are the many young people today who are failing to push for change. The products of the "me" generation and of a self-serving "God bless me" style of Christianity, they have settled for the present mediocrity. Normally young people are more idealistic and radical and are therefore a healthy catalyst for change. They tend to push and challenge the system. This occurred in the late 1960s and early 1970s when many new youth ministries sprang up and Christians experimented with communal living, intentional community, living with a common purse and living in extended households.

In Australia we only need to mention the emergence of the House of the New World, Truth and Liberation Concern, Teen Challenge, House of Freedom and House of the Gentle Bunyip as well as the development of many house churches.

This present youth generation is not working creatively for change and, as a consequence, the ecclesiastical landscape is fairly bleak. The reason why little forward momentum is occurring among youth is a complex social phenomenon which we cannot analyse here. It is my prayer that young people will recover a vision of the radical Jesus and will be able to translate that into new ways of being church and impacting on the world. While I am not suggesting that change can only come from young people, it is my hope that the content of these pages will challenge them to rise up, for it is they who carry the seeds of what the church in the next millennium will be like.

Notwithstanding what I have said earlier, I dare to hope that some of what follows will be relevant to theologians, clergy and denominational leaders, and that they, too, will be encouraged to work for strategic change—to create a church that truly empowers people and releases them for fruitful ways of service in society.

Some thankyous are in order. I am especially grateful to the many outstanding but unsung Christian men and women that I have known personally who have refused to "play church," but have instead sought to express more authentic ways of being Christian and being the people of God. I am also most appreciative of the encouragement and help that I have received from John Waterhouse and Ken Goodlet of Albatross Books. Their interest in publishing a book such as this is in itself a sign of hope.

Finally, I owe much to Chris Brown, who has not only given valuable initial feedback, but has also journeyed parts of this book; and to Jubilee Fellowship, which continues, however slowly, to push the boundaries of what it means to be church.

Charles R. Ringma
Brisbane and Manila, 1994

INTRODUCTION

Talk about church is never easy since church means different things to different Christians. While some strongly believe that the church should adapt itself to changing social realities, others equally strongly believe that the church's structures and form should not change. So to talk about church can be an invitation to controversy.

However, to be critical of the church is even more difficult. For some this demonstrates a lack of spirituality. "How can anyone criticise the house of God?" is their concern. For others, the attempt at criticism is sheer arrogance. "How can any person know what is best for the church?" is their comment.

A CALL FOR CHANGE

My response to both sets of criticism is that what you love you must take seriously even to the point of being willing to criticise it. Dietrich Bonhoeffer once made a comment to the effect that loving one's country means being willing to fight it in order to defeat the oppressive rule that it exercises over others. He was referring, of course, to Nazi Germany.

I believe that the church is also often an oppressive structure and our love for it should motivate us to work for creative change.

My task, therefore, is to engage you, the reader, by demonstrating some understanding of your context, issues and concerns regarding these pressing matters. At the same time, I must attempt to move your thinking along with mine. I see my task as not only to identify and describe the familiar, but also to question, to probe and to propose new ways of being, acting and responding.

Thus, we need to think critically together. This does not mean that I have all the answers, but I can perhaps pose some new questions and attempt, in a limited way, to find new answers. This creative working together of writer and reader does not necessarily mean that readers embrace a writer's answers, but that they also begin to struggle with the questions. If this occurs on the part of the readers of this book, I may confidently expect that more comprehensive answers will emerge.

Meaningful change never occurs single-handed. It is when the many say "enough is enough" and begin to work for alternatives that major changes can occur. But this usually implies that there are those who are asking the questions, identifying some of the issues and tentatively experimenting with new models.

Having said this, it must be emphatically pointed out that I am not proposing a simple, new structure that will make church more authentic and will solve its problems. Solutions are not found in this way. There is no single "prophet" who knows it all. For this reason, I will be speaking about the *contours* of the coming church, not its final shape. And I am suggesting that we change the rules, not merely implement new procedures and methods based on the old rules.

A most glaring example of this failure in our immediate past is found in much of charismatic renewal. At the heart of its theology is the idea that all God's people are empowered for ministry by the Spirit and that each person's contribution is required to build up the church. As a consequence, new ways were found for people to express their giftedness, including their participation in the worship services. But the old rules remained intact, with the pastor holding enormous power for determining the church's life and direction.

Change must be more than peripheral. It must be central and, therefore, must affect power and control issues. In order to tackle these complex matters, participatory, not prescriptive processes are required. So the fuller answers must come from the reader. My questions hopefully will generate new questions on the part of readers and my partial answers will prompt these fuller answers.

Some of the most basic questions are: "How can we move the church from its preoccupation with institutional to people concerns? How can we empower people to take responsibility for their tasks in such a church and in the world?"

Thus, this book is not an invitation to view a blueprint, but a call to a process of change. Hopefully, it is a common commitment to change that will bring writer and reader into collusion.

RESPONSES TO A CALL FOR CHANGE

The danger, of course, is that writer and reader can easily part company on this very point. As a consequence, the envisaged "common journey" of questioning and moving towards possible solutions is aborted at the very beginning.

This occurs because some would argue that change is not called for. The way we presently understand and practise church is the way it should be. Those who hold this perspective usually justify it by an appeal to some authority: "Our church conforms to New Testament practice" they say. Or, "the way we practise church is in conformity with our credal position." While the Lutheran and Reformed churches reflect the latter position, many renewal churches are illustrative of the former.

The basic idea is that we have already got it right because we have accurately worked out our theology. The problem with this approach is that good theology does not necessarily translate into good practice.

Others appeal to the authority of historical development: "This is the way God has led his church to this point in time and this development needs to be respected."

While this approach celebrates God's providential care, it can easily become a commitment to fatalism. It can easily be a celebration of the *status quo* and this throws the sole responsibility for what the church is back in God's court.

Still others point to the authority of some special revelation: "God has shown our leaders that this is the vision for the church and only those who embrace this vision truly belong to the church."

This is the approach of most sectarian groups. Being part of a special group with a special theology makes one a member of the only true church. And, of course, the only true church is that particular group. Sadly, sectarian attitudes exist not only among the traditional sects such as the Jehovah's Witnesses, but also amongst evangelical fundamentalist groups and certain groups within charismatic renewal.

The thought of change amongst such groups is preposterous if not blasphemous, for change would gainsay the nature of the revelation around which the group is built. To call that into question means virtually the disintegration of such a group.

While such people would argue that change is not called for, others herald its necessity, but are pessimistic regarding positive outcomes. They see that change is required, but lament its dismal progress. Given the difficulty of institutional change, significant change in the church will always be stifled, they claim. While some change may occur at the margins, the central power structures will simply continue. Working for change is thus an invitation to frustration.

A case in point is the contemporary women's movement. Being admitted to the pulpit and the administration of the sacraments does not mean that women have necessarily gained significant power. Much less does it mean that the people have gained power to determine their life together in Christian fellowship and their task in the world for mission and service.

Fortunately, others who also see change as important are a little more optimistic. They note that change in the church is inevitable. In this claim, they have history on their side.[1] The different models of being church that the New Testament talks about are quite dissimilar to the churches of the post-Constantinian era, and the church of the Middle Ages bears little resemblance to the church of the present era. The Roman Catholic Church of today is different from that of last century. And the way evangelicals express their way of being church in the 1990s is not the same as in the 1950s. Change has occurred.

Willard M. Swartley has adequately demonstrated how the contemporary evangelical community has changed its perspectives on the issues of slavery and sabbath from those held last century and its perspectives on war and women from those held only a few decades ago.[2] These changes in perspective have had significant implications for changes in the church itself. We need only think of the more significant role of women.

That change has taken place is self-evident. The more relevant question is whether further change is needed. The theme of this book is predicated on a resounding "yes."

THE NEED FOR PROACTIVE AND CREATIVE CHANGE

My observation from history is that the church does not easily and readily embrace significant change. It has to be almost dragged into it by historical factors. While the Reformation was a significant religious phenomenon, it did not occur in a vacuum. Both the Renaissance and the changing political and economic face of Europe helped to provide the setting and contributed to the far-reaching changes in the church. The Reformation might never have happened had other historical events not prompted it.

The church has tended to change only at the point of crisis. This has occurred both in revival and renewal movements such as the Wesleyan revival, and in such difficult political circumstances as the Confessing Church in Hitler's Germany and the blossoming underground church in Communist China.

Seldom, however, has significant change, flexibility and adaptability been an *intrinsic* part of the life of the church. That this is so is amply illustrated by the major and multiple minor splits in the church. The splintering of the Christian community is often primarily caused by resistance to change rather than by doctrinal issues.

Yet in a world which is changing so rapidly, the church needs to become more adaptive and responsive to the social changes that are taking place. For example, it is foolish structuring the life of the church in such a way that does not take into account two highly differing social realities that now characterise many Western countries. On the one hand, we have the underclass consisting of those who are unemployed and underemployed, and the "leisure" class consisting largely of those who have retired. These have time to spare. On the other hand, we have those working demanding jobs, involved in further training and usually with spouses in employment. These have little spare time.

The church obviously needs to respond very differently to these two groupings. Sadly, the church frequently maintains its traditional programs.

The most basic flaw in the maintenance of traditional programs is the failure to distinguish the difference between the essence and the form of the church. One could define the essence of the church as the community of the faithful who are centred in Jesus Christ. The form of the church has to do with the various programs that express the church's essence. These programs should change in response to changing circumstances. The essence of church should not. Sadly, form and essence are frequently confused.

This book is based on the premise that change should be more than inevitable. Change that is forced upon the church by the sheer weight of historical necessity is not creative change. It is reactive.

I am calling for a proactive stance. It is important to change ahead of time. And now is such a time.

THE NEED FOR CHANGE NOW

My readers who claim that such change is not called for may rightly question how I know that now is such a time. As a partial answer, let me make three responses. The first is personal, the second historical and the third a reflection on changing ideologies.

The first (and weakest) argument is anecdotal. Over the past ten years, I have spoken with many people who have left the church. I used to half jokingly, half seriously comment: "Give me all the Christian dropouts and I will have the biggest church in the city." The sad reality in all of this is not only that this would be the biggest church; the churches in general have become like a revolving door—people in and people out. Hence, there is a growing concern that some features of Western Christianity are supermarket spirituality.

Some left the church through sheer frustration. A creative but unusual friend of mine tried to introduce innovative youth programs to a rather conservative middle-class church in the midst of a changing neighbourhood, with working-class and alienated young people—all to no avail. Finally, he set up his own youth welfare organisation and grew several churches out of the organisation's impact on youth. This kind of story could be repeated many times.

Others left having been hurt and alienated by the very institution that seeks to bring help and healing to people. I think of one lady who was counselled by the church to remain in a most destructive marital relationship which led to her serious emotional and mental breakdown. These stories are also a dime a dozen. But, sadly, each one is a person's life.

It is so easy for the church to set up unrealistic expectations for people. Instead of the church being a community of people who are on a faith journey, it so frequently gives the impression that it consists of those who have arrived. Instead of the church being the forgiving community, it can easily become the demanding community. Instead of the church having its arms open to the world, it is often rather like an exclusive club.

But in my experience, none of the above was the predominant reason for people leaving the fellowship of a church. Most claimed the church was no longer relevant. This I think is the most damaging criticism. This means that the church is not so much making mistakes; instead, it has lost the plot. It is no longer scratching where people are itching. It is no longer connecting with the felt needs of people.

While this is true of a wide range of people, it is surprisingly true of the very people the church thinks it serves best—middle-class professionals. Working in the rough and tumble of industry, welfare, law, business or academia, professionals claim that church is tame, timid, bland, safe. They have repeatedly pointed out to me that the church inadequately assists them for their task in the real world.

I have also met with dozens of clergy who have resigned. Each story was different and some were tragic, but they contained a common theme: "The system doesn't really work. It has to be propped up. I have to make it happen and, as a result, the people aren't truly empowered."

Some important issues underlie this common theme. The most basic is that some clergy feel powerless in the very institution in which they play a leadership role. A further issue is that they are labouring under the expectation that they have to perform successfully for things to work. But, unfortunately, their very success—resulting often in burnout or at least overwork—is the very thing that mitigates against people in the congregation playing a larger role and taking more responsibility.

The second response to my questioners is historical. Most of the renewal movements in the church of the 1960s and 1970s have run out of steam. The social justice, community and charismatic renewal movements now bear the marks of rigidity.

This should not come as a great surprise. Sociologists from Max Weber on have piled up research demonstrating that times of change quickly lead to periods of consolidation. It is a well-known historical observation that, after the revolutionaries, come the bureaucrats.

Most of the alternative Christian communities of that time have not survived. Many of those that have survived are now strongly guided by their own traditions. They are no longer creative.

But the best example of the process of formalisation is what has occurred in much of charismatic renewal. One needs only regularly to attend Sunday morning pentecostal services to realise that the first impressions of spontaneity are wrong. Services are, in fact, highly routinised.

These groups are now in need of change themselves and their claim to be at the creative cutting-edge lacks the ring of authenticity.

Even the occasional call to return to their own pristine beginnings is misplaced. Such a time cannot be recaptured, except in the dreams of those who are afraid to move forward and embrace a new future.

My third answer to those who feel that there is no further need for change is a reflection on the ideological changes in this final decade of the second millennium of the Christian era. Key to the worldwide political shifts that are taking place, as well as the current reappraisal in philosophy and the social sciences, is the move beyond ideology. The old systems no longer work. The old ideologies are no longer credible.

This is seen in the gigantic collapse of political Communism which was preceded for decades by the disintegration of major features of the Communist ideology.

One example of this collapse of traditional ideological systems that I am closely acquainted with is in the human services field. People now question aspects of the medical model and want a greater say regarding what is done to their own bodies. The blind belief in the wisdom of the medical practitioner is fast waning. In many areas of life, we have experienced the benefits but also the tyranny of the expert. We want more power over our own lives. This is the time for greater personal responsibility.

The issue of wanting more power over our own lives lies at the heart of the change that I see is needed in the contemporary church. It therefore lies at the heart of this book.

In our highly technologised and politicised world, the role of the lay person has been virtually negated. Experts rule our lives. They even control our psyche. Religious experts often exercise an even greater control because they deal with eternal matters. The most critical change that I believe is needed in the church is for people to have greater responsibility for their spiritual development and for the life of the church.

This constitutes the positive thrust of this book. I am not interested in focussing negatively on the weaknesses of the church. Instead, I am arguing why change is necessary so that people will be empowered.

If we liken the modern world to a sea, there's a wild wind blowing. Too often in the history of the church, when the wind blows, people batten down the hatches and huddle below deck, anxiously praying for the storm to pass so they will stay warm, safe and dry.

But this storm will not pass. This book is written from the conviction that the only way to handle it is to run before it. If we do, we will quickly be surprised to find that Jesus is already out there in front of us, walking on the water in the very centre of the gale. And, like Peter did long ago on the Sea of Galilee, he's calling us to cross the gap and come to him.

The church cannot and will not remain the same. It is attempting to discern the church's future direction that forms the substance of this book.

ENDNOTES

1. One needs to read only Eric Jay's *The Church: Its Changing Image Through Twenty Centuries*, SPCK, 1977, to realise the significant movement of change over the church's long journey.

2. Willard M. Swartley, *Slavery, Sabbath, War and Women: Case Issues in Biblical Interpretation*, Herald, 1983.

CHAPTER 1

A PERSONAL JOURNEY OF CHANGE

Where the markers have pointed me

I am more comfortable discussing ideas and strategies for the church than my own experience of it. Another reason for hesitating to tell my own story is that I recognise that each person's experiences of church are so different that I have at times doubted the usefulness of telling my own story.

So why then give this personal interlude? Would I not do better to weave in the stories of other people with whom I have talked? Or better still, should I not restrict myself to the theological and sociological reflection on the church that forms the substance of this book?

This approach would sit most comfortable with me, but lacks some integrity. For this book is not written simply out of theological and sociological reflection. It has also come out of experience. It is largely the product of a long and often painful journey, and both theology and sociology have come into play to help make sense of that journey.

So I have decided to include this segment, but with several qualifications. First, I intend to be brief rather than extensively biographical—I will refer only to markers of significance in my life. Second, since it is neither my desire nor relevant to be negative about particular churches or denominations, I am going to generalise certain parts of the story so that these groups won't be readily identifiable.

EARLY MEMORIES OF CHURCH

I was baptised as an infant and was nurtured in the church as much as at my mother's breast. Up until my teens, going to church seemed as normal as going to school or playing soccer. It was part of my regular world as were family Bible reading and prayer.

But as much as church was a normal part of my life, it was also totally uneventful. I do have memories of a magnificent Christmas tree brightly lit up next to the pulpit and of the powerful notes pealing forth from a large floor-to-ceiling organ. But mainly there remains with me a blur of unintelligible sermons from men dressed in black. Most of my church time was spent thinking about what I would do once I was outside. Often that revolved around spending and respending the money I had failed to put in the collection plate and considering what the deacons did with the buttons and peppermints I had put in.

During all that time I didn't feel particularly close to God. And I certainly did not feel holy or different. The Bible stories didn't particularly impress me. And imitating Jesus never entered my head. The only thing that made any sort of impact was seeing a Brueghel-style painting in a friend's house depicting those on the narrow way to eternal life and those on the broad way to damnation. It was a hellish painting and struck fear in my tender soul.

I do have strong memories of everyday events from childhood fights in the school playground, watching my brother half drown in the canal, seeing horses butchered in the slaughterhouse, stacking hay in the barn, ice skating and the magic of the Wednesday market day in the town plaza. The images are many and powerful. Those of church are bland.

Even the move from the dank shores of a devastated post-war Holland to the light and sub-tropical spaces of *Australia del Espiritu Santo* made no difference. There was no spiritual light in my experience of church. Unlike many others who drop out of church in their mid-teens, I stayed. But I knew that I was not a Christian. The experience of God had totally eluded me.

Though socially gregarious and active, I was also reflective. Several years of soul-searching ensued, but to no avail. There were no answers to my rather tortuous questions. This brought home my first basic lesson. The church as the mother of faith had failed to succour me.

CONVERSION, NURTURING AND EARLY YEARS OF CHRISTIAN WORK

I came to faith in Christ outside the church I had grown up in. Sadly, the church was not happy with my spiritual experience and dismissed it as due to evangelistic emotionalism. Though remaining in the church, I was nurtured elsewhere. Lunchtime Bible studies and prayer times with people from many denominations in various parts of the city where I worked provided encouragement and growth. This brought home to me two further lessons: the church is so much bigger than one's own denomination; and informal forms of nurture and care are as valid as those organised by recognised denominations.

The experience of church outside the formal church structures occurred in several other ways. One was in my work with Australian Aborigines. The other was in my first pastorate.

My conversion led to a desire to be involved in full-time Christian ministry. The first opportunity was with a mission some years later. There, I witnessed a strange church practice. Aborigines happily came to church when all was well, but they stayed away in droves when there were personal problems. When there had been a gambling or drinking spree, the church was virtually empty. Sadly, this meant that the dominant image of church for them was that it was only for "good" people. One couldn't be a "sinner" and still come to church. On the other hand, it made pastoral work somewhat easier, for one always knew what was going on.

However, this demonstrated that formal churchgoing did not reflect their normal lives. Consequently, much of "real" church happened informally. It was around the night campfires eating kangaroo tail and damper that church really happened. And when whole families moved with the seasonal work of shearing or harvesting to various outlying areas, we moved with them.

Under night's starry canopy, with the distant howling of the dingo and the crisp night air moving in from the even more distant desert, we sang the songs of faith, prayed and listened to Scripture, draped as we were in blankets, and gathered around an ineffectual fire-bucket which couldn't give us enough heat. Here, no-one was absent. Here work and faith met. Here, we worshipped God as creator and redeemer.

The other experience came years later in my first pastorate in outback Australia after completing seminary training. In one sense, my wife and I tried all the right things: pastoral visitation, relevant preaching and special ministries for the children. But what fired people was none of these things. It was the open house discussion and Bible study night that drew all sorts of people including those who weren't even remotely connected with our church.

It seemed that people were looking for what Henri Nouwen was later to call a "safe place." In a room with a crackling wood stove, copious quantities of coffee and cake and an open atmosphere of acceptance, people felt free to share their struggles and joys, relate those to Scripture and bathe them in prayer. And this was not simply the domain of women. Hardened men of the land—fencing contractors and farmers—readily joined in.

CHURCH EXPERIMENTATION

It was soon after this that the journey with the church of my birth ended. The experience of charismatic renewal and the desire for adult baptism which I felt should have followed my experience of faith could not be tolerated by that church, not even after discussion and careful reflection.

Since my experience of the Spirit did not come by way of a pentecostal or charismatic church, I was now ecclesiastically homeless. This left me bewildered more than angry, hopeful more than discouraged. Maybe this provided the opportunity to explore other ways of being church? With my church career already in tatters, maybe something new could emerge from this experience of marginalisation?

The following years were anything but easy and the journey based on experience rather than a closely thought-out plan. But several important things stand out. The first is that our faith was sustained through fellowship with Christian friends. Thus, the home rather than the church was the locus for Bible study and prayer. Second, our experience of marginalisation thrust us into the world for mission and witness. I began working on the streets which was to lead years later to the establishment of the Teen Challenge ministry in Australia. And third, we began to reread church history in order to discover other ways of being the people of God in the world. We avidly read about the Anabaptists and the Moravians and discovered that virtually throughout church history there has been in existence the broken line of a much more radical church alongside that of mainline Christianity. Had Donald Durnbaugh's book, *The Believer's Church*[1] fallen into our hands at that time, he would have saved us much of the searching and study.

This looking to the past had nothing to do with trying to recreate past traditions. It was much more an attempt to gain hope and inspiration for future possibilities.

These three themes—the importance of friendship, the reality of mission to the world and openness to the wider tradition of the church—were to characterise much of what we pursued in the ensuing years and up to the present.

I have deliberately used the word *journey* to describe this process. I don't believe that we ever seriously thought that we would arrive. We didn't dream of utopia and we certainly didn't believe that we would find, let alone create, the perfect church. Moreover, following the writings of Jacques Ellul, we were pretty sceptical about finding the right model of being church. Even the very best institutions that we create frequently need to be subverted later because they have moved away from their initial purpose. Thus, while we kept abreast of all sorts of community developments, we placed little faith in particular structures.

Some of us spent time at L'Abri, others went to Koinonia Farm in Georgia, USA, others visited the Mary Sisters in Darmstadt, Germany, others had exposure to the house church movement, some closely observed Australian Christian community experiments of living with a common purse, and others followed the developments of the Catholic charismatic covenant communities.

We learnt much from all these fine experiments of Christian community. We came to tread a simpler pathway than some of these models, emphasising friendship rather than community *structure*. It seemed to us that Jesus formed a fellowship of friends rather than an institution and that the Pauline house churches were premised more on loving and caring relationships than on particular formal structures. These themes we were later to discover in Emil Brunner's controversial book, *The Misunderstanding of the Church*.[2]

As a consequence, over the past twenty-five years our structural ways of being church have varied. But many of the friendships have remained. Some of the variations included extended households, cluster-housing and a brief attempt at house church at the very beginning. The dominant mode, however, has been small care growth groups with members rotating after a year or so and an extended time together on Sunday afternoons which usually involved worship, prayer, sharing, communion, teaching or preaching, and eating together.

A major structural change over the last few years has been the move away from a corporate eldership model of leadership involving both women and men to a model of rotating coordinators. This move has meant that the whole community is far more critical and integral to decision-making and maintaining community life. The eldership model placed too much responsibility on the leadership and encouraged people to look to them for answers, rather than to assume more responsibility themselves.

The emphasis on ministry has been an integral part of the journey. For the majority of those years, our lives were spent ministering to drug addicts, women in prostitution and homeless young people. A range of diverse ministries was developed. But the common theme was the creation of therapeutic Christian communities to care for and disciple those requesting long-term help.

While these smaller communities of care were first created within the organisation of Teen Challenge, Brisbane, they were later complemented by the extended households and pastoral care groups and Sunday fellowship of Jubilee Fellowship which largely grew out of the Teen Challenge ministry. This allowed young people to graduate out of Teen Challenge and allowed former Teen Challenge staff to maintain tasks and contacts.

While many of the Teen Challenge staff were also involved in Jubilee Fellowship, the common journey continued. But over a ten-year period, Teen Challenge developed more along organisational lines and the relationship with Jubilee Fellowship became weakened.

SOME REFLECTIONS ON THIS STORY

The above story in reality is more complex and should be more finely nuanced. Yet the important features are there. Being brothers and sisters in Christ is to be more than only a spiritual reality. It involves sharing life together. And such sharing involves the voluntary giving of oneself, time and resources. And whether one lives in the same household, or next door, or regularly meets in the same care group, the call to common commitment remains the same.

Moreover, Christian community is not an escape from the world, but the basis for active social engagement. Whatever form that ministry may take—work with troubled young people, with refugees and with strengthening people for their role in the workplace—community forms the basis out of which such involvement can flow. Community is being friends together in Christ in order that we can continue Christ's work in our world.

I don't know whether this story reminds you in any way of the church to which you belong or whether this story is significantly different. What needs to be emphasised is that it is different from the institutional church in that this group owns no buildings, has no paid clergy and most of its giving is given away. It celebrates friendship in Christ rather than a particular form or structure of being church, and maintains a flexibility in ordering its life together.

Change has been and hopefully will continue to be an integral part of its life. In this it is different to the institutional church.

ENDNOTES

1. Donald Durnbaugh, *The Believer's Church*, Macmillan, 1968.
2. Emil Brunner, *The Misunderstanding of the Church*, Lutterworth, 1952.

CHAPTER 2

THE POLITICS OF CHANGE

What makes change so difficult

In the personal journey covered in the last chapter, I did not attempt to picture the ideal way of being church. Instead, I sought to show how marginalisation allowed a group of us to explore different ways of being church. I now believe, in hindsight, that this is a luxury that the institutional church seldom affords its leaders and members. The emphasis there is on continuity. For us, the focus was experimentation.

However, I do not believe the clichéd dichotomies that one frequently finds in a discussion such as this apply here. For example, I do not believe that small is necessarily beautiful and that large churches have all the problems. Not only can a small group have many problems, but it can also be highly authoritarian and inflexible.

Nor do I make the contrast between community and institution, although I strongly believe that church should have the characteristics of community much more than those of institution. But again, we all know that communities can become heavily institutionalised. We need only think of the Amish in Pennsylvania, USA, or the history of monasticism.

Instead, I have sought to show that groups of Christians can adopt various ways of being church depending on ministry focus, needs and composition of the members and the changing circumstances in which they may find themselves. For, after all, the New Testament does not give us *one* model of being church. The communitarianism of the Jerusalem church was not exactly the same as the Pauline house churches, and both were different to the church pictured in the pastoral epistles. I have sought to emphasise that change is possible and achievable.

Furthermore, change is desirable. Unfortunately for the institutional church, change is a burdensome threat. It is the preliminary exploration of what makes change so difficult that forms the substance of this chapter.

THE AUTHORITY AND POWER OF THE CHURCH IS THREATENED BY REAL CHANGE

Many will readily agree that the church does change over time and that the church in this decade is different from last century. The Mass is now conducted in the vernacular and the evangelical church is a much "brighter and happier" place.

These and many other changes are important and should be welcomed. But they are not fundamental. Most of the basic ways of being church have simply continued. This is because religious systems have a great capacity to legitimise themselves and because institutions operate best on the impulse of self-perpetuation.

It is when some of the more basic structures are questioned that we begin to see how difficult change is. At that point, we enter the arena of the politics of change. Change is never only about truth. It is not simply about what is best. It is far more complex than that. It also has to do with politics. And church politics is about power, privilege, status and continuity.

We cannot afford to be naive about the way in which change takes place or is resisted in church. Change should be a matter of moving ourselves and others to live more authentically as God's people in our world. Instead, it is often a power game, where tradition wins over relevance and where present structures block new possibilities.

That change is difficult in the church should not take us by surprise. This is because the church has a thoroughly human face and runs the full gambit of human foibles. It is God's idea, but church is also a human institution. And human institutions frequently lose their way. Over time, they develop a self-perpetuating life and culture of their own. They develop powerful traditions, hierarchies, experts, resources and legitimacies that are hard to resist and change. More seriously, institutions frequently fail to live out their own stated goals and purposes and fail to serve the very people they were meant to serve. And most disconcertingly, institutions can propagandise their clientèle, controlling their lives at the point of their vulnerability, and thus create dependence.

For those who need further convincing about the institutional nature of the church but shy away from reading theology or sociology, Morris West's gripping tale *Lazarus*[1] will leave the reader in no doubt that the church is a heavily encumbered institution.

All of this is not to suggest that institutions are wholly bad and that other forms of association are wholly good. While sociologically we may distinguish a cult or a sect from an institution, I am not suggesting that cults do not experience the above problems. They also control peoples' lives and create dependence—and often much more so! The point, however, is that we *expect* cults to do these things and therefore we are wary of them. We expect that institutions are not like that and therefore we are unsuspecting.

Yet in much more subtle ways, many institutions are not open and flexible. This can also be true of the traditional church.

CHURCHGOERS DO NOT FEEL SAFE EXPLORING NEW IDEAS

In entering the arena of the politics of change, the first thing we need to realise is that much of the impulse for change is lost because the "ordinary" churchgoer does not believe that what he or she is thinking or feeling is legitimate. Such a person may readily think, "I'm not the minister" or "I haven't done theological training, so I don't have the expertise."

This self-negation is frequently compounded by the fact that many churches do not create a legitimate and safe place where concerns or new ideas can be expressed and explored. Sunday services are for worship, teaching and edification; pastoral care groups are for prayer and mutual care and support; and the annual general meeting reports on what the leaders have done—none of these generally provide a place for questioning or debate. And none invite the "layperson" to make his or her contribution to the forward planning of the life and direction of the church.

A safe place is a place of trust. It is the place where everyone's voice is respected. This does not mean, however, that everyone's opinion is or should be acted upon. The safe place always calls for prayer and careful discernment and strategic determination of priorities.

Now it is true that you can always go to your parish priest, pastor, elder or community leader to express concerns or ideas. But if you do this too frequently, you are soon branded a difficult person or a troublemaker. Or at best you are regarded as someone who wants to run the show. If you take this a step further and mobilise others regarding your concerns and ideas, you are usually seen as someone who is undermining the life of the church and resisting God's appointed leaders.

When these types of difficulty occur in the church, the tendency on the part of the leaders is to batten down the hatches and to exert further controls. Yet these kinds of situations can often be avoided when leaders create mechanisms for ventilation and for greater participation.

In all of this, I am not seeking to legitimise the role of perennial whingers—those who can't work cooperatively with others and those who find everything wrong with others except themselves. Rather, I am pointing to the need to create safe and legitimate places where the people of the church can explore new ideas, raise their concerns and be responsibly co-opted to work for the change that they are seeking. While such processes may appear to be messy, they tap the resources of the people and make them co-responsible for the outcome.

For some, the creation of such a safe place is particularly difficult. This is because they believe that under God they alone are to lead and guide the people. The people are not to determine the life and direction of the church. The role of the people is to partake of the life of the church and to support it. This is usually portrayed as a theological issue. This is the way, it is claimed, that Scripture portrays the nature of leadership.

But usually there are other contributing factors. Not only do power issues come into play, but the issue of professionalisation also plays a part. Clergy are trained to provide religious services for people. They generally don't see themselves as facilitators and trainers.

But there are other clergy who believe in the participation of the people. People work on church committees. They play a role in worship services. They are participants in a range of church-related activities and programs. They may even have significant responsibility in particular areas. But they don't participate in determining the overall picture. There is no real power-sharing. Their involvement is welcome as long as they serve the institution and fit in with its predetermined goals.

A few clergy may laughingly dismiss the idea that people should participate in determining the life and direction of the church and be co-responsible for the outcome. "People don't want such responsibility," they may point out. "People come to church primarily to be spiritually encouraged and nurtured. They have neither the time nor the inclination for such a demanding task." And with a slightly more cynical laugh they may remark, "But I wouldn't mind having a few more people in my church who would pull their weight. I sometimes think that I am running the spiritual version of a petrol station. Fill 'em up. Fix 'em up. And then after a time you never see them again."

There is accuracy in these remarks. The clergy themselves, however, have been responsible for promoting this supermarket Christianity. Instead of preaching a "bless me" gospel, it would have been better to have lived and promoted a gospel of grace and freedom that leads to commitment and responsibility.

But there is also a gross inaccuracy in such comments. While many clergy would wish for more people who would pull their weight, they would only want them if they helped to keep the system functioning efficiently. They would be less happy if they were change agents.

MANY, MISUNDERSTANDING THE NATURE OF CHANGE, BECOME DISCOURAGED

But the problem is greater than a lack of safe places where change can be discussed and planned and where there is more power-sharing between clergy and laity. A system can also co-opt the impulses for change by absorbing them without significant transformation taking place. This is so because every social system and institution has some inbuilt mechanisms to cope with a certain level of dissent. A good example is the push in some denominations for the ordination of women.

This push has caused endless debate and much politicking. But while it questions male dominance in the ministerial role, it fails to address the more basic question of ordination itself. Thus, while the attempt is made to broaden the structure to include the role of women, the same basic structure is being perpetuated. In fact, this structure is further strengthened and legitimised by this very process. More particularly, once they are ordained, women may well have to play roles in the service of the church that were determined by men in the first place.

This failure to come to grips with changing the fundamental system merely reinforces it. An even more subtle form of co-option has occurred in churches where women are recognised as pastors, but real leadership is still exercised by men.

Many can be discouraged by the failure to understand why such changes as the women's ordination issue don't change things in a fundamental way. They assume that real change is self-evident and that the strategy is simple. When things are not so straightforward and their ideas are not so self-evident, such idealistic people quickly become reactionary and oppositional. One frequently hears, "If changes are not implemented, I will probably have to leave."

This approach is as intransigent as the clergy who say, "The way we conduct church is based on the Bible, and God has given us the sole authority to lead and oversee this church." Both approaches are inadequate. The one lacks a strategy for implementing change; the other resists change.

For change to occur, certain processes must be adopted. Broadly speaking, it is better that dialogue occurs rather than confrontation and that collusion takes place rather than opposition. More specifically, change is more likely to occur when leadership and people can work cooperatively and common goals can be identified. But for significant change to take place there must be movement in the wider social system. In other words, if change is attempted merely at the local church level but not at the denominational level, then change may be short-lived.

Unfortunately, the institutional church does not welcome change. This failure has produced an "under-class" in the church. This "under-class" consists of people who go to church, but who don't really want to be there. They go out of habit or guilt, but are frustrated, alienated and don't participate fully in its life. This intransigence has also been a factor in producing an "outer-class." While there are many reasons why people leave church, issues relating to inflexibility and authoritarianism are contributing factors.

We are increasingly seeing numbers of churchgoers becoming religious refugees. They have become wanderers in the ecclesiastical landscape. And often such people, rather than finding the energy to start again, have become disillusioned and bitter.

However, this estrangement is not always solely the fault of the institution. It may be that neither the institution nor the person with concerns has created adequate processes for listening, dialogue, reflection, prayer and cooperative strategies that lead to change.

If such strategies are to have any hope of success, then certain further ideas and processes must be put in place. The most fundamental idea is that the people must have a say regarding how they are to structure and share their life together as believers. And the most basic process is that no individual, including the leader, has the final word on what is best for a particular group. What is best must be discerned prayerfully and cooperatively.

MANY WHO COULD CONTRIBUTE TO CHANGE
HAVE GIVEN UP ON THE CHURCH

The pattern in the first part of the 1990s of those frustrated by lack of change has been to leave the church altogether. This is largely negative and unproductive. It is frequently coupled with hurt and bitterness. The people who have left are a lost force which urgently needs to be harnessed. They need to be encouraged to start again. But not on the old terms and conditions.

The pattern of leaving forms a marked contrast to the fundamental impulse of the 1960s and 1970s. Change then was not characterised by leaving, but by creating alternatives. There was room to experiment and an openness to develop new patterns of church life. Much of the charismatic renewal movement operated on that idea and new churches sprang up everywhere. Groups of Christians also experimented with alternative Christian community. And many specialised ministries emerged during that time.

Unfortunately, many of these new churches rallied around a too narrow concept of change. A new form of worship or a new experience of the Spirit formed the basis for a new group. But nearly all the other trappings of the traditional church were taken over by the new group. Sometimes these traditional trappings were pushed to new extremes so that the leaders in these groups became quite authoritarian.

A generous evaluation of these alternatives is that many have become as structured, formal and leadership-driven as the traditional churches. These attempts at alternatives have not shown the way forward. There was change, but it was not radical enough. The old soon reappeared and sometimes with greater vengeance. It is little wonder that people now remain immobilised or leave rather than attempt something new.

Previous attempts at doing something different just don't look too attractive.

This is not to deny that some experiments at Christian community and house church have not only valiantly journeyed on, but have continued to be signposts of hope. Nor does the above overlook the fact that new green shoots are sprouting in the cracks of the asphalt in the form of experiments with base ecclesial communities.

But this is largely leaving the institutional church untouched. Within its sacred walls there is little call for change. One of the most basic reasons is that we have pampered a whole generation of Christians. Brought up on a gospel of cheap grace that promised everything but finally failed to deliver the goods, this "bless me" generation lacks moral backbone. Expecting much and having given little, it has neither the courage nor the vision to work for change.

Sadly, this has left us in a time warp. With the more radical Christians of the 1970s failing to influence the young of the 1980s and early 1990s, with conservatives failing to stave off disillusionment as the wheels began to fall off the "bless me" bandwagon, and with those who had something to offer being marginalised as religious refugees, it is little wonder that the present religious landscape is a vacuum with little sense of forward direction.

It should not be surprising, therefore, that more and more Christians are moving to a private form of spirituality. Institutional Christianity is seen as a hazard rather than in positive terms.

THERE IS NO GROUNDSWELL DEMANDING CHANGE

I have touched on the politics of change before considering the necessity of change because it is vital to realise that change is not simply about new visions, but also about appropriate strategies.

Contemporary sociological literature is replete with theories about the way in which change takes place in society and in organisations. It also spells out strategies for effective change. At a very minimum, these strategies should include open and participatory processes, should allow people to develop their reasons for being together and their statement of mission, and should involve people in owning and taking responsibility for the things they hope to achieve.

But there are few clamouring for change at present. Some have little confidence in their own thoughts and feelings. Some have been marginalised. Some co-opted. Others have left. And the majority remain immobilised.

Many from certain churches question that change is necessary—their churches are growing in number and they are confident that God is blessing them and this land because of them. But the cracks have even begun to appear in this kind of triumphalising. And some clergy from these churches realise that numbers have not translated into commitment and that blessings have not resulted in discipleship.

Fundamental change in the church is now necessary and urgent.

ENDNOTES

1. Morris West, *Lazarus*, St Martin's, 1990.

CHAPTER 3

An Appeal for Change

What is needed in church life

Change involves politcs. To put that somewhat differently, change involves using strategies. Significant change seldom occurs simply and spontaneously. But understanding something of the politics of change does not provide the motive to work for change. What galvanises people is a sense that things should be and can be different.

Since working for change is always a difficult and sometimes a dangerous business, people need to be energised by a vision of new possibilities. These new possibilities, however, need to be more than just ideological. People are seldom galvanised by a great idea that has no relevance to their immediate existence. The vision of new possibilities must be seen by people as legitimate and desired. But it must also resonate with them. I hope in this chapter to find this resonance with my readers.

But the call for change is still weak in many parts of the church. As noted earlier, all the struggle regarding women's issues in the church has only strengthened its institutional nature. The changes I will be advocating are much more fundamental and radical.

This call is not a trumpet blast rallying men and women to a new cause, a new certainty, a new dogma or a new religious experience. Instead, it is a haunting call like that of the night curlew with its eerie cry that unsettles and disturbs.

We do not need a new cause. We certainly don't need a program. And a new religious denomination would be a terrible caricature of what this call is yearning for. So often in churches we have seen the splintering effect. A new group is formed around a new doctrine, around a new form of being church and sometimes around a particular personality. And one only needs to read Helmut Richard Niebuhr's *The Social Sources of Denominationalism*[1] to realise that often the real reasons are not the stated reasons for this splintering. The stated reasons are cast in very pious language. The *real* reasons may be sociological. What I am proposing is not so much the creation of new structures, but the transformation of the old. It is not a call to a new program, but to new processes.

What then lies at the heart of this plaintive cry? The answer will not be the old clichés: more prayer, more evangelism, more commitment, more genuine community and more costly service. We have numbed a whole generation of Christians with these kinds of appeals.

The reason these responses will simply not do is not because they are unimportant; it is because they cannot come by way of demand, but only as a fruit. They only emerge when other things are in place. One of the most basic ingredients is that people need to be a part of the decision-making processes that call for greater commitments on their part. It is what these other things are that needs to be more fully explored.

In probing why change in the church is necessary and urgent, I will concentrate on three key areas where the church has failed its people: their everyday life, their ordinary witness and service, and their spiritual development. These areas are like three windows into the life of the church. They give a view of its interior which clearly reveals why things are ripe for change.

THERE NEEDS TO BE MORE SHARING OF EVERYDAY LIFE ISSUES

Too much of what happens in church does not acknowledge the daily life of its members. The idea that the "sacred" realities of word, sacrament, worship and prayer are meant to give us inspiration for daily life contains an element of truth—but only when these realities are applied to real life and when the "sacred" and the "secular" interpenetrate.

Let me attempt to unpack this rather terse summary statement. Relevant preaching and Bible teaching, for example, will impact on the life of church members by giving them direction, wisdom, hope and inspiration for their daily life. (It needs to be acknowledged, however, that this is rather difficult in a Sunday sermon for a diverse congregation consisting of unemployed young people, high-powered professionals and the elderly. It is immediately obvious that relevance would be enhanced if particular groups and their needs were more specifically targeted.)

But something much more fundamental needs to be recognised. The world of the church with its structure, tradition, doctrines, liturgy and its officers is not the world in which the laity lives. These two worlds are very different. The one is the world of the "sacred" where there are the certainties about God and where grace and blessings are dispensed. The other world in which I live is the world of uncertainty, change and struggle. This is often the world of questioning about God and where blessings frequently seem to be absent.

In saying this, I am not implying that God is absent in that secular world and only present with the church. Instead, I am suggesting that in the world God's goodness is always the surprise. In the church, it is supposed to be guaranteed. These two worlds are often in collision. Worse still, these two worlds often fail to meet. To complicate things even further, the world of the laity never constitutes one, singular world. That of the unemployed teenager is hardly the same as that of the business person, even though both attend the same church.

I believe that the two worlds should much more fully interpenetrate. Everyday life with its joys and struggles should become more the heartbeat of what happens in the church.

Hans-Georg Gadamer in his *Truth and Method*[2] speaks of a fusion of horizons when two worlds meet. He believes that this is essential in the process of coming to fuller understanding. My horizon, or my world, must be enlarged by the assimilation of the other world.

Sadly, so often the church wants me to assimilate its world, but wants to know little about mine. After all my many years of churchgoing, I am still to hear from the pulpit the struggle of faith and life that so many experience rather than the clichéd certainties from clerics who have lost touch with the real world.

Church is usually a "sacred" ceremony which clergy hope will have some relevance for living a life of faith in the real world. It is high time that we register that such hopes are largely unfounded. Much of what happens at church is repetitive and irrelevant. It is driven more by a desire to maintain the church's doctrinal stand, its particular ethos, its programs or its particular vision than by a concern to make the hopes, aspirations and struggles of its people central.

Let me illustrate what I mean. In some churches, one experiences the regular flow of a particular liturgy. Its constancy is somehow meant to be a rock of certainty in our uncertain world. But often it doesn't connect with the particular struggles and concerns of the church's members. Other churches see their main task as indoctrinating people into their particular theological position. It is hoped that this will provide the church members with an intelligent faith which provides answers for their life in the world. But so often doctrines are the playthings of theologians. They fail to be the bread and butter of life of ordinary churchgoers.

In yet other churches, people are made to feel that being a good Christian involves being busy with the church's programs and projects. Now I am not suggesting that liturgy, theology and practical service are not important. What I am concerned about is that people are drawn into the concerns of the church institution and that the concerns of people are marginalised.

Moreover, the church is often more interested in telling people what should happen to them; it is not that interested in what *actually* happens to them. It tells people how to live the Christian life; it is not that concerned to find out whether it really works. In other words, there is a lot of cognitive knowledge transfer. The church's officers are not sufficiently in touch with people to know their questions and concerns. Nor are they close enough to evaluate the practical outworking in people's lives of the things that are being taught.

For example, if the churches of the 1980s which strongly promoted the principle of male headship and leadership (and some are still persisting with this teaching) had evaluated the impact of this teaching in many marriages, they would have been forced to re-evaluate. Here, the church promoted principle over the well-being of people.

What frequently happens in our churches is that the real life of faith of the church's members is hidden from view. It is not central to what happens in church. We have inspirational talks on the nature of God's provision; we don't hear the pain of those who are unemployed. We have church seminars on the ideals of Christian family life; we don't get to hear how that works out in practice for families. Little wonder that so many have a quite unrealistic view of the Christian life.

If we want to teach about God's provision, then we need to know what that means both for those who have well-paid jobs and those who can't find employment. More importantly, we need to explore whether these two groups of people have any responsibility towards each other. The question that needs to be faced is: "Does God provide for others through me and, if so, do I have some responsibility towards those who are without meaningful employment?"

Here we need to grapple with the implications of such passages as: "There were no needy persons among them" (Acts 4:34) and "Our desire is not that others might be relieved while you are hard-pressed, but that there might be equality" (2 Corinthians 9:5).

However, in all this there is a more fundamental issue at stake. The church largely operates on the principle of cognitive knowledge transfer. But we all know that people learn best by example and through practice. Ira Shor and Paulo Freire, for example, in *A Pedagogy for Liberation*[3] have ably argued that knowledge is transformative when it engages both text and context.

Many churchgoers hear lofty ideals from stimulating speakers, but they never get close enough to the church's leaders to see how they themselves put into practice family participation, friendship, neighbourliness, care, loyalty and service. In other words, learning comes from the explication of a text. It does not also come from discipleship within a context. Consequently, modelling has become a lost art in the educational strategy of the church.

All of this forms such a strong contrast to the approach that Jesus took with his disciples. As Athol Gill in his *Life on the Road*[4] has demonstrated, discipleship occurred within the context of a shared life together. In many churches, people do not know each other, let alone share a common lifestyle. And clergy in particular are frequently too removed from their people.

Church services are frequently performance-driven, conducted by religious professionals, and only winners are given a voice. Thus what happens on Sundays is carefully crafted and orchestrated. It is like a well-managed stage play where particular emphases are accented, depending on whether a church is primarily into a liturgical, reflective, instructive, celebrative or social concern mode.

I am making two inter-related points here. The first is that I have never heard the cry of the person with a disability from the pulpit; I have only ever heard testimonies of healing. In other words, only certain activities are acceptable.

Second, whole churches are premised on a particular emphasis. Some are focussed on worship, others teaching, others again on social concern. And so you can take your pick. Depending on what you are into, you can find a church to meet your needs.

Now many people would argue that this is, pragmatically, a good thing. I am seriously calling this into question. I do so not because I am opposed to diversity, but because this reflects the very institutionalisation and fragmentation of life I am arguing against. This diversity reflects particular theological emphases and therefore this is once again an institutionally driven diversity. This does not reflect the wholeness of life that church members experience.

Since it will not do to hide reality in order to be inspirational, it is time that the gathering together of Christians provided the opportunity for the ordinary issues of life to be shared, and for these issues to be brought to the Bible for further light and bathed in prayer for enlightened action. People's issues and not the church's agenda need to predominate. Thus sacred and secular realities can interpenetrate and we can hear the cry of those in pain as much as the testimony of those who have experienced God's healing power.

In the shared time when Christians meet, more needs to be heard about financial pressures; people's struggles in a difficult economic environment; women's roles at home, at work and in the church community; the tension of following career paths and involvement in Christian service; issues of isolation and boredom in a society that all too quickly makes the elderly redundant; the experience of loss; difficulties and pressures at work; spending quality time with our children. More needs to be heard about how people pray, spend time in reflection, read Scripture and are encouraged by particular books. And more needs to be heard about how people are involved with their neighbours; how they have made links with the wider community; how they are seeking to bring the light and love of Christ to their part of the world; and how they are responding to the bigger issues of injustice and poverty in our world.

The above suggestions are in no way programmatic. They are merely suggestive.

Many other and much more basic suggestions can be made. If we can hear in the worship service from young people about their successful beach outreach during the school holidays, why can't we hear from them about a wonderful party they have had? If we conduct weddings and funerals, why can't we celebrate birthdays or graduations? And why shouldn't we hear from the Asian migrant about the struggles of fitting into a new society, making that central to our worship service? After all, the Bible is full of texts regarding strangers and sojourners.

To put all that somewhat differently, Jesus constantly wove important teaching around the ordinary life experiences of people. He took a child and spoke about the importance of a particular style of leadership for the Christian community (Mark 9:33-37). So why can't we hear from a person with a disability about the experience of marginalisation and make that a theme for a particular service?

Terrence Tilley in *Story Theology*[5] points out that stories provide the substance of the Christian faith. What I am arguing is that our story and that of the Bible's should more dynamically intersect.

If we are not hearing from each other regarding these and many other of life's daily issues and possibilities, then we are not sharing life together. If our lives only touch in a building where we hear inspiring preaching or experience uplifting worship, but we know little of how things are working for us on the ground, then our lives remain hidden. The rich resources of our various experiences as Christians in many walks of life and in the seasons of life's journey are excluded as a valuable reservoir of learning and encouragement.

This is a tragic loss. While adult education is premised on utilising the life experiences of its students, much of the church's program fails to utilise these experiences. The church tends to operate in a parent-child mode rather than as a community of equals.

This failure to tap into the rich texture of human experience with all its triumphs and tragedies has not only made much teaching narrow and unrelated to practice, but has also made much theology irrelevant. Much theology is now the province of the Studies in Religion department of the university rather than the seminary. This location has removed theology from the heartbeat of the Christian community. Consequently, theology has become the learned discussion of academics amongst themselves and is preoccupied with methodological issues—yet they nevertheless attempt to dictate what the church should believe.

They claim to provide a theology *for* the people of God. Instead, they should develop a theology *of* the people of God where the faith, experience, service and reflection of the ordinary people of God are articulated. Here books such as Robert Banks' *All the Business of Life*[6] provide a promising initiative with its central idea that theology should concern itself with all of life and not simply with an interior spirituality, and that the theological task should be deprofessionalised.

Church should celebrate the actual experience of life of its members, not some idealised and sanitised version of it. Since the people are the church, it is their journey of life and faith in the light of Scripture that should be central.

THERE NEEDS TO BE GREATER ACKNOWLEDGMENT OF INFORMAL WITNESS AND SERVICE

The second window through which we see the necessity of change is the church's failure to acknowledge and make central the many informal ways of witness and service that are occurring.

A telling example is where a church committee develops a special plan for service and action by the church in the community and then tries to sell it to church members for their involvement and support. Such a project may vary from a series of special meetings with an outside speaker to the development of a pre-school program for neighbourhood children. The possibilities are in fact endless. It is this plan that receives all the publicity, the prayers and the church's money. This is the official project. But no thought is given to establish what church members are already doing in their neighbourhood and places of work.

No attempt is made, for example, to identify the medical practitioner who has changed the approach to patients by providing counselling and practical support rather than just curative care. No attempt is made to identify the local councillor in the congregation who is tackling certain important quality of life and social issues in the community. No attempt is made to support the lady who is conducting an informal neighbourhood Bible study group. No attempt is made to support prayerfully the teacher who has just started work in an inner-city school with many pupils from broken families. And no attempt is made to see one family's care for their disabled child as a ministry worthy of the church's support and prayers.

This list could be extended to include as many people as there are members in church: a young person's role as school captain and her commitment to care for all the students, but especially those from migrant families; a businessman providing quality employment including those who are training in job creation schemes; a father on a school committee who is wanting the school to be progressive, but also wishes to see high moral standards developed; parents providing foster care and their struggles in helping children overcome the dysfunctional character of their previous families; a lecturer being genuinely available to students and the implications this has for her lack of time for research and publishing; a young person working as a volunteer in a youth refuge and the pain in knowing that many of these young people will simply end up back on the streets with no permanent place to call home.

All this and so much more speaks of the reality of the people of the church throughout the week in their places of work and training and in their neighbourhoods, with all their social contacts. It is a kaleidoscope of opportunities and possibilities, a rich tapestry where ordinary life and Christian service join, not in a clash of contrasts, but in a harmony of colours.

And why is all this not central to the church's mission in the world? Why is this not supported? Why is this not celebrated? Because the church operates on promoting the "special." Its own special programs and projects, often determined only by the church's leadership, are the focus of the church's mission in the world. The beauty of the ordinary, of what is *already* informally being done, is not acknowledged—perhaps because it cannot be controlled and no organisation can receive the credit.

The tragic implication of this is that the church operates an agenda that pushes the multitudinous expressions of the people's love and service to the margin. Only the church's formal areas of service are considered legitimate. The people's work as the "scattered" church is not supported and remains unacknowledged.

This further illustrates the extent to which church is institutionally driven. While this may sound hard, it is written with tears and great sadness of heart. The church is not for the people. The church is for itself. By this, I mean that it is preoccupied with its own institutional life, its own continuity and its own agenda.

Let me illustrate with a story. Someone came to faith in Christ through our ministry with troubled young people. He came to help, but instead found the pearl of great price. We encouraged him to link up again with the church from which he had strayed several decades earlier. But instead of this church encouraging him to continue in his obvious gift of working with young people, they drew him onto various church management committees. They co-opted him for their own ends. Today, while still a Christian, he is alienated from the church which sought to exploit him.

There are even more blatant forms of church being for itself. The worst is where church leaders take a whole group of people down the suspect pathway of a particular theological hobbyhorse, an expensive building program or particular ministry project that has mainly to do with satisfying the competitive ego needs of church leaders and little to do with serving the needs of the people.

Here, we don't need to think of the suicidal spiritual eccentricities of a Jimmy Jones or a David Koresh. We can think of ordinary ministers who have exhausted their people with some grandiose church growth project, or others who have led people into the esoteric belief that they have some final truth and alone are the true body of Christ.

It is high time that we acknowledged that churches don't always do good things to people. Some churches, like families, are dysfunctional. They exploit people's guilt or vulnerability and make them dependent, rather than empowering them for responsible life in the world.

THERE NEEDS TO BE MORE STRESS ON SPIRITUAL DEVELOPMENT

In the very area where one would expect the church to do well, it is doing badly. This is the area of spirituality. Spirituality here means much more than conversion, coming to faith in Christ. It is also more than the disciplines of prayer and meditation.

Spirituality is the Gestalt of one's Christian life. It is the ethos by which one lives. Spirituality cojoins inner motivations and outward actions. Spirituality summarises one's inner life and one's lifestyle.

In some areas, the church is doing well. One example is in the area of Sunday "entertainment." The evangelical church, for example, is a much brighter and happier place. Not only is there enthusiastic chorus singing, but also fine solo renditions and good Christian bands. There is nothing dull about going to such a church. In the area of social services, the mainline churches have also generally done well. These churches have developed hospitals, schools, services for the aged and for those with disabilities as well as ministries to prisoners and those who are socially alienated. All of this is commendable.

But the church's approach to spiritual formation is abysmal. The issue is not that Christian writers have failed to deal adequately with this subject. One need only think of the extensive writings of Thomas Merton, Henri Nouwen, Thomas Green and Richard Foster that deal with the development of spirituality in general. There are many wonderful resources that deal more specifically with spiritual growth and development, and its relationship to stages in the life cycle, crises, sexual differences and temperament. And there is a plethora of books on how to be a spiritual director who assists people in their spiritual formation. The problem is that the church does not use its own resources.

One reason for this failure is that spirituality is approached from the perspective of church as institution. In some churches, confirmation, confession of faith and baptism are emphasised; in others, conversion leading to a public testimony, baptism and Spirit baptism form the pivotal points of one's spiritual development. In some churches, spiritual formation is seen in terms of strategies of soul-winning and methods of service.

But what is lacking in all of the above is the development of appropriate strategies that help people to develop a holistic Christian lifestyle—that joins prayer and work, worship and sexuality, family and community, reflection and action, church and world. When this is lacking, the church is operating on the faulty presupposition that spirituality is somehow caught rather than taught. The assumption is made that, providing one regularly attends church, partakes of the sacraments, hears the preached word, prays and reads the Bible, one will grow into spiritual maturity. A further assumption is that this will occur in a fairly smooth linear development.

Both assumptions are flawed. Spiritual maturity needs to be formed in the midst of life as much as in the midst of the church. And spiritual development is never the smooth transition from darkness to light, from infancy to maturity and from disorientation to integration. Spiritual development is much more cyclical and dialectical. Sometimes, we have to recover what we have learnt earlier. And sometimes old lessons need to be reintegrated.

While I in no way wish to underplay the importance of meeting together, learning together, participating in the sacraments, praying, and listening to and reflecting on Scripture, I do not believe that mere institutional participation in these processes leads to spiritual maturity.

In fact, the opposite is the case. An institutional dependence on these things guarantees immaturity. If I am well socialised into the ethos of the church, this does not necessarily prepare me well for my participation in the world. In fact, it could make me take a world-denying stance. And, as I believe spirituality is the co-joining of my inner and outer world, it is imperative that my spirituality is formed in both the church as well as in the world outside the church.

Spiritual formation occurs in the warp and woof of life. It begins when I take responsibility for my spiritual development and when I stop using the church as a spiritual cafeteria. It develops when I put into practice the things I am learning. And, as I respond to life's challenges and opportunities, I will learn from experience much more than from mere hearing.

Allow me to unpack some of the points I am making. First of all, *I must stop using the church as a petrol station*. It is not the place where, having run down my spiritual energies during my Monday to Saturday week, I come for a fill-up. I must be responsible for my own spiritual growth. After all, my spirituality is not simply mediated to me by the church. I stand in a personal relationship with Jesus Christ and have received the Holy Spirit as a gift. It is incumbent upon me that I foster that relationship. Consequently, I come to church to participate, to share, to join with others, to use my gifts. I don't come only to receive.

Second, if I am to take responsibility for my own spiritual development, then *I need to practise what I am learning.* And this practice must extend beyond the church. It should include the family, the school, the workplace and the neighbourhood. Practice stimulates one's spiritual development and these experiences can be shared when the community of faith gathers together for encouragement and edification.

Third, life is not some smooth and even experience. It is full of twists and turns. We all know times of joy and difficulty. Our spiritual development requires more than the safety of the church. It is more fully shaped in the ups and downs of life.

My spiritual development, moreover, will be enhanced when I take risks, live boldly the life of faith and prayer, begin to take on the courage of my convictions and live with some integrity. It is furthered when I face life's disappointments, deal with ambiguity, come to terms with contradictions, overcome anger and bitterness, acknowledge my pain, use my gifts and accept limitation.

What I am suggesting is that *our spiritual development* should not simply be adequate for our role, tasks and involvement in the world, but *should be forged in the midst of life.* For it is there that I experience fear, am tempted to compromise and avoid situations that require commitment and action. It is there that I need to face my pain and seek to work for peace and reconciliation.

While church can teach me some of the principles that underlie the above, it cannot adequately train me in these realities. It cannot take me by the hand into the world. It can only send me forth into the world. But what the church is often failing to do is to provide me with companions on the journey. Also, it is failing to create opportunities for feedback and further encouragement and direction.

Here, the church functions as a typical institution which provides certain services and goods, but does not create a community of persons who share a life together. It teaches me about the importance of prayer, meditation, solitude and service as critical to one's spiritual growth. But there is no laboratory of life—there is no shared lifestyle. There is no being in solidarity as we work out in the world the things we are learning.

Sadly, the church as institution does little to encourage people's spiritual formation in this way. It is not geared to deal with training people for life's diversity and is not structured for community building processes.

Simply put, spiritual development should be holistic. It should be more than the promotion of an interior spirituality of faith and prayer. It should also include our service in the midst of life. But the church cannot teach such holism if it is structured as an institutional reality. It can only do so if its people share life together, learn from each other, encourage each other and walk a common journey. A fragmented setting such as the institutional church cannot shape people for all the business of life. It can only provide religious ceremonies which hopefully will help people in their task in the world. Such hopes, I have suggested, are unfounded.

In this chapter, I have identified three areas that need changing in the church. These areas are not incidental or peripheral. They are fundamental. They are three windows through which I have chosen to look into the church's life.

We could also look through other windows; in fact, it is important to do so. We could learn from observing how decisions are made in the church and how power is exercised. We could also learn from those who have left the church. Furthermore, we could learn much from building up a picture of what people still in the church actually believe and do. It would probably not correspond all that much to what leaders think that the people believe and do.

What the three windows I have chosen indicate is that church is institutionally driven and that people have little power and few ways to make their concerns and contributions central to being church. Few things could be further from the vision of the people of God that emerges in the New Testament than this.

Clearly, the gap between Jesus and the church is very wide indeed. If we are going to "catch the wind," change is imperative. We need to look closely at how it can come about—at the basis for such change, some of its processes and what a changed church may look like.

ENDNOTES

1.Helmut Richard Niebuhr,*The Social Sources of Denominationalism*, Charles Scribner's, 1929.

2. Hans-Georg Gadamer, *Truth and Method*, Seabury, 1975.

3. Ira Shor and Paulo Freire, *A Pedagogy for Liberation*, Bergin & Garvey, 1987.

4. Athol Gill, *Life on the Road*, Lancer, 1989.

5. Terrence Tilley, *Story Theology*, Michael Glazier, 1985.

6. Robert Banks, *All the Business of Life*, Albatross, 1987.

CHAPTER 4

THE BARRIERS TO CHANGE

What issues make us baulk

I have suggested that change in the church is both necessary and urgent. It is necessary because church has become too institutionally driven and fails to make central the life and concerns of the people it is meant to serve. It is urgent because people are being alienated.

Some of those experiencing alienation are clergy. Alienated clergy feel that they can no longer maintain a form of church where everything depends on them. This is particularly true of clergy who have experienced burn-out. They have come to see that they have been unable to be the amazing spiritual all-rounders who could meet every expectation. And they now lament the fact that they were unable to mobilise people for participation and responsibility.

Others experiencing alienation are church members who have begun to question the way things are done. They are ahead of the current church's practice. These people are frequently skilled in various disciplines of the social sciences and practise participatory processes in their work environment. They know about participatory leadership, team building and group processes, and are appalled at the outmoded and often reactionary ways in which the church does its business.

Others again, seekers, those in search of spiritual values, find church a difficult place because it demands a commitment to its goals and values rather than inviting people to a journey of personal growth and spiritual discovery. What all too often happens with this group of people is that the church too quickly demands a commitment to its doctrines and meetings. Instead of allowing seekers ample time to understand what the Christian faith is all about, the church too readily pushes for closure. In so doing, it either pushes people away or it forces them to make a premature response.

Karl Rahner, in his book *The Shape of the Church to Come*, argues that the church should be open rather than a boundary-centred group which concentrates on defining who is an insider and who are outsiders. Moreover, he suggests that sympathisers, those who relate to the church but have not committed themselves, should be regarded as part of the church rather than as strangers.

People come to faith in Christ in a variety of ways and their development is most helpful when they can move at their own pace. The church should therefore create an open environment for people to do their searching, ask their questions, experience the life of Christians and so come to an intelligent commitment rather than a forced one.

Because people are being alienated, it is imperative that we address the question of change in the church. The call for change, however, invites the question: Can *we* change the church? Many would argue we may not—that only God can change the church. I insist that we must. It is *our* responsibility.

IS NOT CHANGING THE CHURCH GOD'S PREROGATIVE, NOT OURS?

It is argued by some that since the church belongs to God, he alone has the right and power to renew and change it.

There is much truth in this position, but it is one-sided. It is true that the church belongs to God. It is true that people of all times and places who have responded in faith to the living God—the God of Abraham, Isaac and Jacob who has revealed himself in the face of Jesus Christ—are part of God's church. It is also true that God by his word and Spirit calls people to faith, to share in a common life focussed on his Son and to serve him in our world. And it is true that God by his providence and great love sustains and cares for his people.

What is not true is that the particular form and ethos that the church takes is without human instrumentality. While God is responsible for the church's essence, we are significantly responsible for its form. We shape the church's institutional reality. We create particular forms of leadership, doctrines, disciplines, liturgies and programs.

Let me illustrate from history. During the first century of the Christian era, the church functioned as a charismatic community. The emphasis was on people using their gifts for a variety of ministries. By the second century, this focus was being undermined with the emergence of the role of the monarchical bishop. The shift from ministries to offices was a phenomenon that people created. Similarly, the move from the house churches of the Pauline mission to the development of church buildings set aside especially for the worship of God is a historical, man-made development.

Another example is provided by looking at present forms of church leadership. These have more to do with contemporary management models than with the New Testament. The leaders of the Pauline house churches were exercising a function and utilising a spiritual gift. They were not holding a particular office. Moreover, these churches operated on the principle that all had been gifted by the Spirit and were encouraged to exercise their gifts for building up the Christian community.[2] Leadership in the contemporary church is positionally based and has to do with delineating a range of duties and responsibilities. This is what we have created. It follows that if present leadership characteristics are made by us, we should also be allowed to change them.

It is stating the obvious that we create the church's programs. It is we who decide that the church must have a choir, Sunday school and special youth program. It is less obvious, perhaps, that we create our own doctrines. But it is true. The history of theology indicates that particular doctrines are shaped in response to major social and political forces of the time. Jacques Ellul in *The Subversion of Christianity*,[3] for example, notes that in times of a unified monarchy God is seen as king, and in times of chaos and disruption he is seen as father.

What we create we are responsible for. It is these aspects that we should feel free to change since God holds us accountable. If we ourselves have made many of the traditions, rules and regulations of what we now call church, we have every right to change those aspects of church. And we are *obligated* to change them when we see that they are no longer relevant or helpful.

For example, if we see that large church gatherings leave significant numbers of people uninvolved and the church fails to disciple them, then it becomes imperative to create other structures that will facilitate Christian growth. Howard A. Snyder, in his *Liberating the Church*,[4] argues that with the disappearance of a general Christian consensus in many Western countries, it is urgent that the church becomes a counter community where Christians can develop a shared lifestyle that does not become submerged by secular values.

Central to the matter of accountability is the idea that the form of the church must approximate its essence. If the essence of church is the sharing of life together through Christ's reconciliation, then that reality must be reflected in the church's structures and programs. If the essence of church is based on an equality that Christ brings so that women and men, black and white, poor and rich have equal status by his grace, then such a reality should be reflected in the leadership structures and the form of the Christian community.

Given the above, the church of the same denomination can't have a nice white middle-class church in one part of town and a struggling black church several blocks away. This convenient arrangement violates the essence of the church.

Similarly, one can't believe the above and have only male clergy. If one of the fundamental concepts of the New Testament communities was the breaking down through Christ of social and cultural barriers,[5] then clearly all can play a role in the community. Women can be leaders. Laity can administer sacraments. And rich and poor need to find ways of finding an equality of lifestyle.

Essentially, then, my argument is this: it is God's prerogative to maintain the essence of the church; it is our responsibility to make sure that the structures we create reflect the heart of God's intention for his people.

This summary statement has important implications. It means first of all that we can't settle for any sort of change and certainly not for change for change's sake. That is a luxury we simply cannot afford. Second, it means that the change we should work for resonates with the heart of biblical revelation. It is change that harmonises with the liberating impulses of Scripture regarding the Christian community.

Thus change in the church is not simply God's prerogative; it is also ours. But there can be no doubt that when we acknowledge that essence and form belong together and that God's intention and our structures should harmonise—and then work for change accordingly—that God's Spirit will be actively involved in such a process.

The task, then, of bringing about change is ours, but it is not ours alone. God's Spirit jealously broods over the church seeking to guide its life. Our efforts for positive change, while sometimes fraught with difficulty because of human resistance, can also be marked by the Spirit's blessing.

WOULD NOT CHANGING THE CHURCH VIOLATE CERTAIN UNSHAKEABLE ELEMENTS?

Some people are concerned that working for change in the church may change what should not be changed. Christians from various traditions claim that certain elements of the church are inviolate.

For the early church fathers of the second and third centuries, two important elements of church were the role of the bishop and the church's sacramental life. The idea developed that the monarchical bishop constituted the centre point of the church's life and the eucharist was regarded as the food of salvation. These two elements were integral to an understanding of church at that time.

For the pre-Reformation Roman Catholic church, what was essential had much to do with the church's hierarchical reality. The Catholic theologian Avery Dulles, in his book *Models of the Church*,[6] points out that this understanding of the church emphasises a hierarchical conception of authority which patterns itself on the way jurisdiction was exercised in the secular state. Dulles goes on to point out that this overemphasis on institutionalism is a deformation of the true nature of the church.

For some of the Reformers, the unshakeable elements of church had to do with the pure preaching of the word of God, the administration of the sacraments and the practice of discipline. While John Calvin, for example, emphasised that the church was the mother of all the godly and that the church is a living organism and a communion of mutual service, he nevertheless focussed on the formal aspects of word and sacrament. And as Wilhelm Niesel[7] points out, Calvin added the role of discipline. While Calvin held that Christ is the soul of the church, discipline serves as its sinews by which the various members of the body of Christ are held together.

For some Anabaptist groups, the unshakeable elements of church focussed on community and pacifism. Picking up on the matter of community, the Anabaptists emphasised that the in-Christ relationship produced the horizontal reality of community. As Robert Friedmann points out,[8] the Anabaptists elaborated the brotherhood concept of church where brotherly love translated into cooperation and the sharing of material resources.

For some contemporary Christian communities, the non-negotiable element of church is holding disposable income in a "common purse." Trevor J. Saxby, while emphasising that the sole foundation of Christian community is Jesus Christ, insists that in such a community, sharing must be complete and that all things must be held in common.[9]

This list could go on and on. What is obvious from these few examples is that the important elements *vary* between the different groups. This suggests that it is very difficult to establish certain external criteria and make these the hallmark of the church. There are problems with saying, "If these things are in place, then we truly have church." For in reality, *all* these criteria may be in place, but we may still be a far cry from being church.

Failure to be church adequately may have many causes. Usually our irreducible elements are too narrow. Dietrich Bonhoeffer, among others, has roundly criticised the Reformation teaching on the marks of the true church because it failed to emphasise the importance of *koinonia*, or fellowship, as an essential element of what it means to be church. Bonhoeffer emphasised that there is no area of the church which is not wholly and exclusively subject to Christ—that it is a dreadful reduction of the New Testament concept if today the church is often seen to have its existence only in preaching and the administration of the sacraments.[10]

Frequently our criteria become, over time, rigid formulations without life-giving reality. The century following the Reformation saw the rise of Protestant orthodoxy where perspectives became hardened and rigid and the church, instead of being the herald of grace, became the embodiment of legalism.

And finally, some of the criteria that we develop arise out of particular historical needs and situations. The formation of the class or the small group in John Wesley's revival was a response to the social dislocation that many converts had experienced and aspects of the Salvation Army's way of being church (such as no sacraments) was an outworking of the target group of people they were working with, and sprang from a desire not to antagonise other churches.

The broad observation from history is that once a particular feature of a church's life is set in place in its formative period, it tends to become a permanent fixture. It is difficult to conceive, for example, that the Presbyterians will change their pulpit-centred approach to understanding church or that Anglicans or Episcopalians will change the priority of liturgy.

Yet the church must change with the times. Thankfully, today's school is no longer like the school of fifty years ago. Not only is the school environment different, but educational strategies have changed. The same is true of our hospitals and many other institutions. Positive and constructive change should also occur in the church. Not only does the church over time need to use different metaphors to explain its life and vision, as has occurred in the Roman Catholic church with its present image of church as the pilgrim people of God, but it also needs to change its structures and priorities.

In an age when kings were the order of the day, it was perhaps appropriate to speak of the church as a kingly and ruling institution. In a democratic and pluralistic environment, it is probably far more meaningful to speak of the church as a counter-community. However, the pressing issue is not simply the change of metaphor, but the change of sociological reality.

It will not do, therefore, to say that we may not change church because it embodies certain irreducible elements. Not only do these elements emerge out of particular historical situations and therefore need to be adapted over time, but they can also become rigid and formalised and therefore no longer serve their initial intended purpose.

Change is always called for, not only in the peripheral areas of institutional life, but also at its centre. Let me give an example of what I mean. The Presbyterians and other Reformation churches centralise preaching and the pulpit. Now clearly the obedient listening to the word of God is a basic element to being church. But in many of the base ecclesial communities (BECs) in Latin America, communal Bible study has replaced the role of the preacher and pulpit. This participatory way of studying Scripture has been found to be more effective than normal preaching.[11]

The historical observation that after the revolutionary thinkers and activists come the bureaucrats is also applicable to the church. God's Spirit, jealous for the essence of the church, works in concert with faithful women and men to renew the church's life and vision; but these impulses are quickly controlled and formalised. Renewal movements in the church quickly develop new leadership, new legitimations, new theology and new structures. The sociologist Max Weber described this as the movement from "charisma" to "routinisation."

In the development of the church of the New Testament, it is obvious that a major shift has occurred by the time we come to the pastoral epistles. The Pauline house churches with their emphasis on gifts and ministries is replaced by an emphasis in the pastoral epistles on offices and duties. Bengt Holmberg provides an interesting study of how quickly routinisation occurred in the communities of early Christianity.[12]

In our day this problem has not gone away. Renewal communities which set out to renew the face of the church within a few years have shown a marked formalisation. Peter Berger and Thomas Luckmann explain this as partly due to people's need for closure and existential certainty.[13] In other words, human beings can cope with some change. But they cannot cope with leaving their options open for too long. When this occurs, they suffer from what sociologists call "anomie," a social vacuum marked by the absence of social norms. Consequently, renewal groups quickly settle down to new certainties and legitimations.

It is because this process of formalising occurs and occurs rapidly that people must change the elements which they regard as capturing the heart of the church. For these elements more often reflect human formalisations than the heart of what it means to be church and they most frequently arise from our human attempts to control and organise.

My point, then, is this: the unshakeable elements that we regard as sacrosanct in typifying church are the very elements that we need to creatively subvert, or at least actively counterbalance. While we may think that we have discovered these elements in our quest for truth, they have more likely emerged from our desire to control and stabilise.

Thus when we have discovered the importance of the word, we may need to rediscover the value of celebration; when we have discovered the relevance of community, we may need to re-emphasise the importance of individuality; when we have discovered the power of the Spirit, we may need to recover the value of servanthood.

The other important and often neglected element in this discussion is that at the local church level, the matter of what constitutes church is overlaid with all kinds of in-group trappings.

For example, while an evangelical denomination may *formally* emphasise that being part of the church involves faith in Christ, belief in the Bible as the authoritative word of God, confession of faith, baptism, and living a life of holiness and service, at the local level an *informal* agenda may well form the dominant ethos. This agenda may emphasise that faith in Christ involves a particular form of conversion, that the Bible is almost a "magic" book from which we extract promises that suit our lifestyle, and that holiness becomes a withdrawal from life and a preoccupation with externals of dress, make-up and how we spend our leisure time.

What occurs in cases such as these is that the formal marks of the church are acknowledged, but an informal reality reigns. Trying to call that informal reality into question is the bane of all those seeking change, for informal agendas are seldom acknowledged.

Sociologists have long pointed out that institutions operate on two sets of logic. There are the formal operational systems and there are the informal ways of doing things and getting things done. Sometimes, the informal reigns supreme over the formal reality. When change is attempted at the formal level but the

79

informal is not adequately addressed, then some formal changes may take place, but the same informal reality continues.

If significant change is to occur in the church, then clearly both the formal and informal aspects of church must be addressed.

WOULD CHANGING THE CHURCH BE IN OPPOSITION TO SCRIPTURE?

We should not change the church, it is argued by some, because the church is based on scriptural authority and to call for change is to call Scripture into question. This is the predictable appeal of many conservatives who favour the *status quo*. But it is based on spurious logic.

In the first place, there is so much that we do in church that has nothing to do with the New Testament. Many of the church's customs and priorities have simply developed from tradition. There are endless examples of this ranging from our church buildings, our clergy-laity distinctions, most of our institutional trappings and even such trite things as having two services at (often) awkward times of the day and an order of service that is as predictable as a German railway timetable.

Second—and this is much more serious—there is much in the New Testament that we don't practise. Our churches aren't places where rich and poor find a common life in Christ. Instead, we have our well-to-do churches in the better part of town and our struggling churches in the suburbs of social dislocation and despair. Our churches aren't places where everyone can exercise their gifts and make their contribution. Instead, we promote the role of the religious specialist and accept the ministry of the socially acceptable. There is no way in our present churches whereby greater honour is bestowed on the weak, the poor and the marginalised than on others.

We encourage, for example, the public testimony of the rich, the famous, the beautiful or the spectacular, never the "ordinary" people and their struggles. And if the church has to make a choice between establishing a school program for its own middle-class families or developing an after-care program for ex-prisoners, the former project will get voted in.

Third, most church practice is based on selected use of Scripture, not on Scripture as a whole. The more traditional Roman Catholic view of church draws more from the pastoral epistles. As we noted earlier, these New Testament writings focus more on office rather than charismatic gifts and on institution rather than community. Little wonder that this was found to be attractive as the Roman Catholic church developed into a hierarchical and sacramental institution.

Protestant churches, and particularly the Reformed and Lutheran churches, draw more from the *theology* of the Pauline epistles. This is because of their preoccupation with the pulpit and their concern with sound doctrine. The Christian community movement is more influenced by the Acts description of the early Jerusalem church.

More radical Christian communities are frequently more influenced by the prophetical books of the Old Testament and the Gospels in the New Testament. It is not surprising to find that the late Australian New Testament scholar, Athol Gill, rooted his understanding and practice of community in the Gospels.[14] Contemporary house churches draw more from the *practice* of the Pauline communities.[15]

Thus Scripture itself contains a range of models of what it means to be church. We tend to select the model that best suits us. One would indeed be hardpressed, for example, to justify the argument that the Presbyterian model of being church is the only or the best model that Scripture portrays. In fact, it would be easier to argue that this model, with its emphasis on pulpit,

81

catechesis and elders, is more a Reformation development than a return to the ethos of the New Testament, where offices were fluid and functional rather than positional and defined, and where the role of all the members of the Christian community was emphasised.

I believe that the argument of those who hold that we may not change church because it is based on Scripture should be turned around. The catchcry on all of our lips should be exactly the opposite. We must constantly be changing church because of Scripture. Scripture as a whole should call our way of being church into question.

This was the espoused ideal of many of the Reformers with their call that the church must always be being reformed. But this has seldom been practised. Yet practise it we must—particularly because we so easily make church into an institution that we can control and regulate and which finally becomes a distortion of God's ideal.

ENDNOTES

1. Karl Rahner, *The Shape of the Church to Come*, SPCK, 1974.

2. 1 Corinthians 12 to 14.

3. Jacques Ellul, *The Subversion of Christianity*, Eerdmans, 1986.

4. Howard A. Snyder, *Liberating the Church*, IVP, 1983.

5. Galatians 3: 28 and Ephesians 2: 14–22.

6. Avery Dulles, *Models of the Church*, Doubleday, 1974.

7. Wilhelm Niesel, *Reformed Symbolics: A Comparison of Catholicism, Orthodoxy and Protestantism*, Oliver and Boyd, 1962.

8. Robert Friedmann, *The Theology of Anabaptism*, Herald, 1973.

9. Trevor J. Saxby, *Pilgrims of a Common Life: Christian Community of Goods through the Centuries*, Herald, 1987.

10. Charles Ringma, *Seize the Day with Dietrich Bonhoeffer*, Albatross, 1991.

11. For a helpful discussion on this approach to hearing the word of God together, see Carlos Mesters, *Defenseless Flower: A New Reading of the Bible*, Claretian, 1990.

12. Bengt Holmberg, *Paul and Power*, CWK Gleerup, 1978.

13. Peter Berger and Thomas Luckmann, *The Social Construction of Reality*, Doubleday, 1966.

14. Athol Gill, *Life on the Road*, Lancer, 1989.

15. Robert Banks, *Paul's Idea of Community*, Anzea, 1979 is a good illustration of this point.

CHAPTER 5

THE IMPERATIVE FOR CHANGE

What questions demand an answer

In dealing with some of the objections to change, I have already begun to spell out something of the imperative for change: that we have shaped the human face of the church by creating particular forms and structures and we are therefore bound to change them when these forms and structures become irrelevant or oppressive.

A second consideration is that we define the dominant images of church by isolating certain characteristics, yet in time these images are no longer relevant. The modern Catholic Church, for example, no longer defines church primarily as hierarchical institution, but as pilgrim people. Gustavo Gutierrez, writing from a Latin American perspective,[1] insists that faith cannot be lived on the private plane of an interior spirituality. Faith, instead, creates community and such community must express itself in solidarity with the interests and struggles of the poor. Karl Rahner, writing from a German perspective,[2] insists that the church be built up from below in the form of basic communities as a result of free initiative and association.

A third consideration is that the richness of Scripture should constantly call our limited attempt at being church into question. More particularly, we should embrace the principle that the more liberating passages of Scripture should be foundational to our understanding of church. For example, we shouldn't let Paul's discussion on the role and status of women in 1 Corinthians 11 take precedence over his ideal in Galatians 3, verse 28.

Yet there appears to be a deep reluctance when it comes to significant change in church. It is almost as if change is sacrilegious. This is particularly so with the more central elements of church. While we don't mind changing some things about the youth group or the ladies' meeting, we find it difficult to accept that any person in church should be able to administer the Lord's supper or baptism.

This reluctance to face the need for real change makes it essential to look at two fundamental questions: Has the church delivered? Has the church remained relevant?

HAS THE CHURCH DELIVERED?

One important element to pursue is the question of outcomes. The church, like many other human institutions, claims to do certain things for people. These may be called its "mission statement." It is appropriate to ask whether good outcomes are being achieved. And the people to ask are the recipients of the services.

Research in the area of the provision of human services demonstrates that service providers usually define for service recipients what they need and then go on to claim how well they meet these needs. When recipients of services are asked to define their needs, however, they are usually quite different. And when these same recipients are asked how well service providers are doing their job, there is usually justifiable criticism.

This is so because the providers of human services have a vested interest in their own needs and in their own careers. These do not always coalesce with the legitimate needs of the people they claim to serve.

For quite a number of years, I had the opportunity to work as a senior research assistant at the Department of Social Work and Social Policy, University of Queensland. The research team, headed by Chris Brown, evaluated a significant number of non-government welfare organisations in the provision of services for physically and intellectually disabled people. Using an action research model that focussed on consumer perspectives, the research consistently indicated that organisations failed to place as central the legitimate needs and aspirations of clients. In a nutshell, the organisation operated on the premise that it knew what was best for consumers, but it in fact had failed to adequately consult with consumers.

In this regard, church is no different. It, too, claims to know what people need. But, similarly, it fails to consult its people. Moreover, the needs of church functionaries and the needs of the church as an institution may receive a greater priority than the people who both receive and support its services. When this occurs, the church is failing to be a servant of its people.

So let us sharpen the question: Is the contemporary church achieving good outcomes for its people? The answer generally is "No."

There is anecdotal evidence to support this response. Several of my friends left church because of its inability to help them through their marriage break-ups. When the church sided with one of the parties, believed to be innocent, the other left, feeling judged and rejected. One woman friend left church because women were constantly put down and regarded as inferior to men. Several others left because they believed the church's message of success, power and achievement was so much out of step with the Jesus they knew from the Gospels that they could no longer identify with the church's corporate life and worship.

The list could go on. One couple felt that the church was a self-serving institution, while another person felt that it did not empower people, but finally had to do only with clergy power. Another said that the church, through its charismatic leadership and ministries, often manipulates people to believe certain things and to maintain particular loyalties to the group.

But for the majority I have talked with who have left church, the issue has been different. It is the sheer *irrelevance* of what happens on Sunday. So much of contemporary preaching is either second-rate pop psychology dressed in religious garb or it is theologically abstract material. Neither of these are finally helpful. But even more seriously, so much of church is participating in an orchestrated religious ceremony that does not engage the real issues. Church has little to do with people's daily life, their workaday world and their personal struggles and pain. Furthermore, it has little to do with people's genuine aspirations for serving their neighbour and seeking to transform the world.

The contemporary church does not achieve good outcomes for its people because it fails to give them responsibility and keeps them dependent. It provides "sacred" services through specially set-apart "sacred" individuals for ordinary recipients, who need to show their gratitude by giving loyalty to the institution that provides these services. This gives power to the institution and its specialists, but keeps ordinary people in a disempowered position. In other words, the laity knows exactly what it may not do: preach, administer the sacraments and run the church. But the laity knows that it has to be grateful to the clergy who run themselves into the ground doing precisely what ordinary members may not do.

In the delivery of medical or social services, we are told that the specialist knows best; in the church, this is compounded because the minister or theologian is not only the specialist, but has also been "appointed by God." With the provision of religious services by religious specialists, the role of ordinary people is mainly to "purchase" such services, even though they do so by putting money in the plate rather than by paying a fee.

The reference to purchasing religious services seems hard and critical, but it has become characteristic of some parts of evangelical and charismatic Christianity. People go shopping for churches that suit their style. Inevitably, they end up in churches with many specialist services and with high entertainment value. This church is not only a pleasant experience, but there are also "Christian" services available, from creche through to old people's homes.

The implication is not only that one ends up in a Christian ghetto. One also does not need to assume much responsibility for one's own spiritual growth and development. It is all laid on and it generally keeps people quite happy.

One outcome that most churches would seek to achieve for their members is spiritual growth and maturity. But this cannot readily be achieved within the present system, for maturity can only come when the people *are* the church and, under God, assume responsibility for its life and mission.

To put that differently, if the spiritual growth and maturity of its members is one legitimate goal that the church seeks for its people, then the church must adopt appropriate processes for that to occur. A person will not grow into maturity if everything is done and provided. This will only occur when people assume responsibility. However, the church has foolishly locked itself into a position between a rock and a hard place. It continues to provide religious services for people where people remain largely uninvolved and it hopes, at the same time, to grow them into maturity.

When church is the institutionally-driven provider of religious services for the people instead of the life together *of* the people, then certain outcomes can never be properly achieved. When this occurs, the call for change is not only justified; it is imperative.

HAS THE CHURCH REMAINED RELEVANT?

The failure to produce certain outcomes for people provides a basis for change. The failure to remain relevant provides a further basis.

Churchgoers, along with everyone else, are part of the movement of history. There have been times in the life of the church when some of its members have been at the forefront of historical change—when new ideas and a new vision have begun to permeate a society. Some outstanding Christians, for example, were at the forefront of the early development of modern science.[3]

Much of contemporary Western Christianity, however, warrants no such prestigious place. Rather than being at the forefront of social change and progressive thinking, it needs to be dragged into the arena in order to begin to participate.

Many examples could be given of the church's reluctance, but these will suffice. The church has been a latecomer to the area of human rights, it has only belatedly put ecology on its agenda with its "greening" of theology, and it has lagged behind secular proponents of holistic development and community work.

An ongoing difficulty in contemporary Western Christianity that contributes to the above problems is that, in rightly rejecting the theological tenets and practice of liberalism in the early decades of this century, much of the church has remained ambivalent in understanding its role and task in the world. The fast-growing evangelical, charismatic and pentecostal churches still tend to take a world-denying rather than a world-affirming position.

Moreover, some sections of the church maintain a reactionary stance which longingly, but foolishly, looks to a bygone era when the church had special status and privilege in a world that has long ago slipped through its fingers. Bemoaning its loss of a key place in the social and political machinations of a past century, the church has failed to reorganise itself as an incarnational lay and grassroot movement that seeks to build a new society from the bottom up.

What I mean by this is that the church has not forgotten the Middle Ages, the millennium of the *corpus Christianum* where church and state, the Bible and the sword, were the twin pillars of society. In that scheme of things, the church was a highly privileged institution which at times even dominated the state. While the reality of this state of affairs is gone, the dream still continues amongst such contemporary groups as the neo-calvinist reconstructionists.[4]

Rather than pursuing this dream, the contemporary church should rebuild from a position of weakness, not one of imagined strength. It needs to see itself as the "little flock" in a pluralistic world. It should shape its existence on the kingdom values of the New Testament which, as Donald Kraybill has shown, are so different from the normal values of this world.[5] In ordering its life to the tune of a different drummer, the church as a counter-community can once again act as leaven, salt and light in society and inject new impulses of life, hope and transformation into a mortally wounded world.

The church can no longer influence the world from a position of power and privilege, for the church has never handled this position well. Power has only weakened the church and undermined its integrity.

In some sense, the church has to start all over again. It urgently needs to transform its own life and, having done that and continuing to do that, it can give its life for the transformation of a world that has become satiated with its dreams, only to find them a shimmering mirage under a bright desert sun. If the church fails to relinquish the power of the old, it will never be able to work effectively in producing the new.

One implication of all of this is that the church is not in one sense "modern" enough. This virtually reverses the persistent harping of Christian leaders who say that the great threat to the church is secularism. Francis Schaeffer, for example, sees the problem of the church as one of accommodation to the secular consensus.[6] He speaks of the world spirit of our age crushing all that we cherish in its path and concludes that our culture and country deserve nothing else than to be under the wrath of God.

While I agree that secularism, with its emphasis on relativism, materialism and self-seeking individualism, should be ardently resisted, more wholesome modern impulses need to be evaluated and selectively utilised. In other words, everything that emerges in the modern world is not necessarily bad. God is providentially involved in this world. And Christians can learn from the good things in our society. We certainly should not be negatively reactive to everything that happens. On the other hand, we do need to be discerning. But things do emerge around us that Christians can positively utilise.

There are many examples that could be used. Two will hopefully suffice. The one is the feminist movement. The other is the development of self-help themes in human services.

After the more radical and probably less helpful impulses of feminism of the 1970s had faded, a more constructive phase has occurred in the last decade. Feminist Christian scholars have not only addressed the important issues of male and female roles in family, church and society, but they have also contributed to the whole field of biblical studies and systematic theology. A good example of the former is Elizabeth Schüssler Fiorenza's *In Memory of Her: A Feminist Theological Reconstruction of Christian Origins.*[7] A representative example of the latter is *Feminist Theology: A Reader.*[8] To ignore this constructive development will only leave the church further impoverished.

The other example is the theme of self-help. The idea of self-help has permeated most human service delivery. Effective community work occurs when the resources and aspirations of people in the local neighbourhood are identified and utilised. This means that their efforts are part of the solution. In other words, instead of professionals determining what a particular community needs and then doing it *for* the people, the strategy is first to get to know that community and assist them in identifying their key needs and working out what constructive projects should have priority. The further strategy is then to mobilise people in the achievement of the outcomes. Thus community work becomes the work *of* the people, not work *for* the people.

This approach not only means that certain projects are accomplished, but also that the processes involved in achieving those outcomes provide the additional benefits of community building and enhancing the dignity of the members of that community. These types of strategy in self-help are also the key to successful overseas development projects.[9]

Even services for people with physical and intellectual disabilities stress the role of clients in service determination and control. In other words, the traditional model of service for people with disabilities with its emphasis on medical control is being replaced with services that encourage community living and the maximum amount of self-determination. Instead of hiding people with disabilities in sombre institutions, they are now being encouraged to join mainstream society.

Also, in more enlightened medical care which traditionally has been so expert-centred, the role of the patient is being elevated from passive recipient to active participant.

Studies are indicating that people are expecting more preventative education from their medical practitioner. They also expect better feedback regarding diagnoses and more discussion regarding possible treatment options. Put very bluntly, they expect to be treated as reasonably intelligent human beings who have some understanding regarding how their body works and functions.

This movement, which places greater responsibility and self-determination into the hands of "ordinary" people and minimises the controlling role of the expert and specialist, is a movement from which the church could learn. The church could also learn from the women's movement in overcoming sexism.

It is in this sense that the church is not "modern" enough. It is reluctant to pick up creatively new social trends which begin to permeate a culture—and which also influence people in the church. While some of the church's members may see possibilities in these ideas, and while some of the church's leading thinkers may promote them as being theologically sound, the church at large is resistant. It is afraid of adaptation and change. This is surprising for an institution which began as a radical change movement within a tired and legalistic Judaism of the first century AD!

In one sense, it is understandable that the church is afraid of such change. The idea of self-help and self-determination in the life that a group of Christians shares together dynamites the traditional role of church as institution and would radically change the role of the religious expert.

Under such an arrangement, the needs, hopes and aspirations of people become central in the coming together for worship, prayer, listening to Scripture and participating in the sacraments. Moreover, if people are setting the agenda for their life together under the lordship of Christ, then the role of the expert is only advisory and complementary, not determinative as is the case in institutional Christianity.

All of this is not an argument for a "worldly" church or for a secularised Christianity, but for a relevant church. Sadly, we tend to be bad readers of the signs of the times. At worst, we tend to be reactionaries. And to our shame, we adopt these new impulses only when our contemporaries have long ago integrated them and have begun to struggle with other issues. For example, while the battle is still raging regarding women's roles in the church, secular society has put in place equal opportunity legislation which guarantees the role of women in the workplace.

So far, then, I have disagreed with the idea that we should not change the church and suggested two bases for change: the failure to produce certain stated outcomes and the failure to remain relevant and respond creatively to the more positive impulses in our society. But though important, these are clearly inadequate in themselves to justify the call for radical change in the church. More is required.

In fact, nothing less than a rereading of Scripture is called for—a rereading which will provide a new vision for change.

ENDNOTES

1. Gustavo Gutierrez, *The Power of the Poor in History*, SCM, 1983.

2. Karl Rahner, *The Shape of the Church to Come*, SPCK, 1974.

3. For an interesting discussion of this development, see R. Hooykaas, *Religion and the Rise of Modern Science*, Eerdmans, 1972.

4. .See R.J. Rushdoony, *The Institutes of Biblical Law*, Presbyterian and Reformed Publishing, 1973.

5. Donald Kraybill, *The Upside Down Kingdom*, Herald, 1978.

6. Francis Schaeffer, *The Great Evangelical Disaster*, Crossway, 1984.

7. Elizabeth Schüssler Fiorenza, *In Memory of Her: A Feminist Theological Reconstruction of Christian Origins*, Crossroad, 1983.

8. *Feminist Theology: A Reader*, Ann Loades (ed.), SPCK, 1990.

9. For a good example of the many educational strategies that undergird this approach, see Anne Hope and Sally Timmel's *Training for Transformation: A Handbook for Community Workers* (3 vols), Mambo, 1984.

CHAPTER 6

THE SOURCE FOR CHANGE

How the Bible can help us catch the vision

It is Scripture rather than tradition which finally should shape our understanding of what it means to be church. Not everyone agrees with this. Some hold to a developmental approach, which claims that the way God has led the church up until the present is the way the church is meant to be. This approach is basically evolutionary. It is the approach that is favoured by those who emphasise the role of tradition as much as that of Scripture. Instead of insisting that the development of the church in the second and third centuries with its emphasis on bishop, priest and sacramental meal was a distortion of the New Testament, this position maintains that it was a providential development.

I reject this position in principle, for ultimately it does away with a critical evaluative dimension. Moreover, if we overemphasise the notion of God's providential care, then we undermine the part that we play for good or ill in shaping the church.

I believe that the New Testament's role is to call our contemporary views of church into question. My position is a restitutionist one, a "looking back" to a restoration of New Testament principles. A good example of the restitutionist impulse was the Anabaptist movement. It sought to build church much more as a New Testament-type caring-and-sharing community than the mainstream Protestant groups did. Although Martin Luther surprisingly had a similar vision of church, he failed to implement it.

In the preface to the *German Mass*, Luther writes:

> Those who really want to be Christians and to confess the gospel in deed and word would have to enrol by name and assemble themselves apart in some house to pray, to read, to baptise, receive the sacrament and to do similar Christian works. For in such a regime it would be possible to discover and punish and correct and exclude those who do not behave as Christians and to excommunicate them according to Christ's rule in Matthew 18. Here, too, a common collection of alms could be enjoined on Christians to be given voluntarily and distributed to the poor following Paul's example in 2 Corinthians 9. . . Here, baptism and the sacrament could be administered in a brief and simple manner and everything directed to the word and prayer and love. . . In short, if one had people and individuals who really wanted to be Christians, the rules and forms could soon be drawn up.

Instead of pushing for this more restitutionist mode of being church, Luther insisted that the time was not right for this development. He writes:

But I cannot and will not order or establish such a community or congregation yet, for I do not yet have the people and individuals to do this nor, so far as I can see, are there many pressing for this.[1]

Sadly, Luther failed to grasp the nettle and the opportunity was lost due to the subsequent development of territorial churches with their emphasis on institution and the role of the prince to provide legal protection for the church. Moreover, Luther was hopelessly wrong in his assessment that no-one was pressing for a much simpler form of house church. The Anabaptist movement essentially practised what Luther failed to work towards.

Now it needs to be emphasised that the restitutionist position is not a pining for the good old days, nor is it based on the premise that we can exactly recapture the form and ethos of the early church. We not only cannot return to the reality of the ancient world, but we do not want to recapture the social realities that were normative at that time. Who, for example, wants slavery restored?

But what is desirable, I believe, is to recapture the approach that the New Testament communities took in radically responding to the social needs of that time and the way in which they ordered their corporate life as a counter-community. More particularly, it would be worthwhile to recapture not so much the form of the New Testament communities, but their vision for a life of worship, sharing and service.

To do this we need to engage in a critical rereading of Scripture in the light of contemporary reality. This requires some careful elucidation. What do I mean by the words "critical," "rereading" and "in the light of contemporary reality"? This will require a brief journey into the world of contemporary hermeneutics— the art of understanding and interpreting the Bible.

THE VISION CAN BE REDISCOVERED BY A "CRITICAL" READING OF THE BIBLE

A "critical" reading becomes necessary because the Bible is neither a uniform, nor a systematic piece of writing. And the New Testament in particular is best classified as occasional literature. What I mean by this is that the New Testament is written in response to the particular situations and needs of the early Christian communities of the time. These writings do not evidence the attempt to make a final, comprehensive or definitive statement on a particular issue, particularly not on the precise shape of the church. The metaphors used to describe church are many and varied, ranging from "body" through to "family" and "temple."

As a consequence, one cannot say that the New Testament contains one clear view of what it means to be church. It uses *many* images and pictures to describe some of the key qualities of church and faintly outlines several models.

One dominant image is church as the body of Christ (1 Corinthians 12 to 14) with its key concept described in chapter 12, verses 12 and 13:

> The body is a unit, though it is made up of many parts; and though all its parts are many, they form one body. So it is with Christ. For we were all baptised by one Spirit into one body—whether Jews or Greeks, slave or free—and we were all given the one Spirit to drink.

Not only does the Pauline metaphor of church as body of Christ emphasise ideas of unity and mutual participation, but it also stresses radical reintegration. The body of Christ is not a homogeneous group consisting only of Greeks or free persons. It is a culturally and socially diverse phenomenon.

Yet Paul also uses the more structural images of church as household and temple. In Ephesians 2, verses 19 to 22, he writes:

> Consequently, you are no longer foreigners and aliens, but fellow citizens with God's people and members of God's household, built on the foundation of the apostles and prophets, with Christ Jesus himself as the chief cornerstone. In him, the whole building is joined together and rises to become a holy temple in the Lord. And in him you, too, are being built together to become a dwelling in which God lives by his Spirit.

Here the images are different, but the same integrative reality is present. The new community consists of culturally diverse groups who have found unity in Christ.

One model of church is the more institutionalised idea of church as pictured in the pastoral epistles (1 Timothy 3); another is the house churches of the Pauline mission (Romans 16, verses 3 to 5); a third is the Jerusalem community (Acts 2 to 4).

A critical reading of the New Testament must attempt some evaluation of the various images, pictures and models. In other words, we shouldn't allow the diverse images to stand equally without some attempt at integration. This approach, too, must attempt to answer whether there are more perceptive revelatory "moments" in the New Testament and some parts that are less so.

For example, we could ask the question whether the teaching and leadership role that Priscilla took alongside that of her husband (Acts 18, verse 26 and Romans 16, verses 3 to 5) is a more significant description of the role of women than that found in 1 Timothy 3, verse 11 where the wives of deacons are described as needing to be "women worthy of respect, not malicious talkers, but temperate and trustworthy in everything." For Priscilla, there is a dynamic and participatory role in the church. For these other women, no role is envisaged other than that they are to be quality persons.

The idea of more perceptive revelatory "moments" does not deny that all Scripture is the word of God and wholly sufficient for faith and life. It simply accents that Scripture is neither uniform, nor systematic and that it therefore requires careful reading in order to discover its most powerful insights.

By way of further example, we may note that the Pauline manifesto of cultural, social and sexual equality and unity in the body of Christ, expressed as follows in Galatians 3, verse 28 ("There is neither Jew nor Greek, slave nor free, male nor female, for you are all one in Christ Jesus") is not maintained in the pastoral epistles, which emphasise gender and social subordination (1 Timothy 2, verses 11 to 15; 1 Timothy 6, verses 1 and 2; Titus 2, verses 9 and 10).

The verse that probably reflects this position most clearly is Timothy 2, verses 12 to 14:

> I do not permit a woman to teach or to have authority over
> a man; she must be silent. For Adam was formed first, then
> Eve. And Adam was not the one deceived; it was the woman
> who was deceived and became a sinner.

Whether one likes it or not, the reader has to make some choice whether the Galatian material or that of the pastoral epistles is to be the dominant image.

This critical approach to Scripture is not new. It certainly has nothing to do with the old liberal critical approach which denied as the word of God anything in Scripture that did not fit with an anti-supernaturalistic world view. Instead, this approach echoes the old Reformation principle of "canon within canon," which recognised that some portions of Scripture are more radically significant than others. We probably know this principle best from the writings of Martin Luther when he gave the book of Romans priority over that of James, because of the latter's failure to spell out specifically the concept of justification by faith as contrasted to doing good works.

THE VISION CAN BE DISCOVERED BY
A "REREADING" OF THE BIBLE

The idea of "rereading" Scripture also requires some explanation. While Scripture remains the same, our reading of it changes.

As we change personally and as key values in our society change, we will go to Scripture with new questions seeking new answers. Since neither our personal nor our social horizons remain static, we need to grapple with Scripture anew. This means that to a greater or lesser degree the task of doing theology needs to be done again in each generation.

By way of example, no-one today would attempt to mount a biblical defence for the validity of slavery. Some Christians played a key role in its demise through a radical rereading of Scripture, yet most Christians in the past believed that slavery was a God-ordained, social reality supported by Scripture (1 Timothy 6, verses 1 and 2), and that those who denied this interpretation were undermining the authority of Scripture.[2]

A more contemporary example relates to women's issues. With the significant political and social emancipation of women this century, as well as the more constructive impulses of the feminist movement in general and feminist theology in particular, there has come about a significant rereading of Scripture regarding the role of women in the early Christian communities. This rereading has brought to the fore the significant role of women in the Jesus movement (Luke 8, verses 1 to 3); their witness to the resurrection (Matthew 28, verses 1 to 7); their prophetic role in the early church (Acts 21, verses 7 to 9); their role in the early house churches (Acts 18, verse 26 and Romans 16, verses 3 to 5), and their significant role in the Pauline mission (Romans 16, verses 1 to 16).

What these verses and others indicate is that the early Christian movement was not predicated on the solo role of men. While the pages of the New Testament bristle with the exploits of men, a more careful reading indicates that the part that women played is everywhere significant. It is as significant in the Jesus movement as in the Pauline mission.[3]

When the above passages on the role of women in early Christianity are linked with the Pauline manifesto of the new equality in Christ (Galatians 3, verse 28), this rereading of the New Testament has resulted in the rejection of the old position of women's subordination and marginalisation. This has brought women of today into the mainstream life of some of the more progressive churches, including into the roles of leadership and teaching.

The example of the emancipation of women also illustrates what I mean by the rereading of Scripture "in the light of contemporary reality." The significant social shift in the role of modern women has caused us to reread Scripture with this question in mind: What has the Bible to say about the place and function of women in the early Christian communities?

This question has led to the recovery of the vision that in both the Jesus movement and the Pauline house churches, the role of women was far more significant than first thought. This new understanding of the role of women in early Christianity has had an impact on our perception of the role of women in today's church.

THE VISION CAN BE REDISCOVERED BY A DYNAMIC READING OF THE BIBLE

The hermeneutic that underlies the above thinking is the dialectic of the two horizons.[4] The key idea here is that we never come to Scripture in a neutral fashion. We always come with the pre-understandings of our contemporary horizon, with the presuppositions of our context and with the questions of our time. As society changes, our presuppositions and questions also change. Or if we relocate ourselves in a different social context, our questions will of necessity be different.

This is why liberation theology, for example, which has arisen out of the oppression experienced by the Third World's poor, has a very different theological focus from theology in the First World. While the latter is concerned with the question of meaning in a world characterised by relativism, Third World theology is concerned with liberation in the face of oppression and poverty.

To put that differently, the social location of the First World has produced a very different theology to that of the Third World because its concerns are different.[5] Much of the theology of the First World continues to be a response to the enlightenment, where reason supplanted faith and revelation, while in the Third World the pressing issue is not the problem of reason, but the issue of survival in a world of poverty and injustice.

As a result, different theological themes have emerged in the Third World. The most fundamental theme is that God is not the God of philosophical abstraction with its emphasis on his eternity and omniscience, but is the God who has entered the human arena to side with and liberate the poor. This liberation is not merely a spiritual transformation, but includes social reality. Hence the exodus theme is an important paradigm for liberation theology.[6] Even liberation theology's greatest critics will admit that the Third World's rereading of Scripture from the perspective of "the wretched of the earth" has opened up new understandings regarding God's concern for the poor.

This dynamic, hermeneutical approach that I am advocating, however, does not mean that our contemporary concerns control or dictate to Scripture. This is where this approach differs significantly from the old liberalism, which made contemporary concerns determinative for Scripture's horizon.

The old liberalism with its low view of Scripture and its high view of modern progress was far too optimistic regarding how significant change could occur. It virtually identified social change with the kingdom of God. It, therefore, minimised the Bible's call for radical conversion and spiritual transformation. As a result, it undermined the supernaturalism of Scripture and judged it in the light of modern values. This way of understanding Scripture advocates no such thing. It rejects both humanistic optimism and that our horizon can dominate Scripture. Thus the direction is completely reversed to that of the old liberalism. Our horizon raises new questions, but it is Scripture that provides the answers.

A simple illustration regarding the interaction between the two horizons should suffice. Several centuries ago, women's issues were not a concern. A woman's subordinate role was simply accepted in both society and the church. Since the end of the nineteenth century and particularly since the 1960s there has occurred a monumental shift regarding the status of women. This shift in our social horizon has forced biblical scholars and theologians to look again at what the Bible has to say about women. And after decades of research, the picture has emerged that Scripture has a far more positive view of the status of women than first thought.

Now one may object that this proves the opposite of what I am seeking to establish. It shows that the Bible is subjected to contemporary ideas. Here, it may be claimed, the modern horizon predominates, not that of Scripture. However, I believe this has not occurred. While the shift in our social horizon has forced scholars to ask new *questions* of the Bible regarding women's issues, the *answers* regarding a more balanced view on women have come from Scripture itself. From the Genesis emphasis that both women and men are made in God's image and have the task of rulership, through to the role of women in the Jesus movement and the Pauline mission, the evidence is strong that women enjoy equal status to men in Christ.

It follows that sometimes new questions that arise from our contemporary horizon lead to new answers. Asking new questions that arise out of our contemporary reality can awaken meanings and perspectives in Scripture which have been there all the time, but which were submerged or neglected.

ENDNOTES

1. Wilhelm Niesel, *Reformed Symbolics*, Oliver and Boyd, 1962, p.253.

2. See Willard M. Swartley, *Slavery, Sabbath, War and Women: Case Issues in Biblical Interpretation*, Herald, 1983.

3. See Elizabeth Schüssler Fiorenza, *In Memory of Her: A Feminist Theological Reconstruction of Christian Origins*, Crossroad, 1983.

4. See Hans-Georg Gadamer, *Truth and Method*, Seabury, 1975.

5. See Jon Sobrino, *The True Church and the Poor*, Orbis, 1984.

6. See J. Severino Croatto, *Exodus: A Hermeneutics of Freedom*, Orbis, 1981.

CHAPTER 7

THE VISION FOR CHANGE

What new insight can transfrom the church

The vision now to be presented is the central theme of this book. It arises from understandings that contemporary society gives us about ourselves and the church, and which open new horizons on the Scriptures.

People empowerment

Using Thomas S. Kuhn's notion of a paradigm,[1] we may formulate this issue as follows: the shift that has begun to take place in our contemporary horizon that is causing us to ask new questions about the nature of the church is the issue of *people empowerment*.

At one level, the theme of people empowerment may bring to mind Gandhi's mobilisation of the masses to achieve India's independence, Dr Martin Luther King's campaign in the USA for black civil rights, or the more recent EDSA revolution in the Philippines which resulted in the overthrow of the Marcos dictatorship.

But the notion of people empowerment is far more pervasive than those major public events. It is the result of a confluence of many factors.

In philosophy, it is the recognition of the important link between experience and understanding. In education, it is the recognition of the link between doing and learning. In theology, it is the growing emphases on orthodoxy (right belief) and orthopraxis (right action). In community and development work, it is the connection between self- help and social change. In psychological literature, it is the link between responsibility and growth.

To fully unpack this summary statement would lead us into a major discussion of the philosophy of such writers as Hans-Georg Gadamer and Paul Riceour, the educational strategies of people such as Paulo Freire, contemporary theologies such as liberation, black and feminist theologies, community studies such as *Training for Transformation*, and the psychology of writers such as Rollo May. Such a discussion would be too far-reaching for a book that is focussed on effecting change in the church. However, this summary statement does require some elaboration.

At the heart of people empowerment lies the concern that our modern world, with its emphasis on bureaucracy and technology and its attendant emphases on structures, procedures and experts, has undermined the legitimate role of individuals. Despite the rhetoric on human rights and equal opportunity, people today find themselves to be victims of the larger economic and socio-political forces in the world, a tale most poignantly told in Tom Wolfe's novel *The Bonfire of the Vanities* and more philosophically explained in Jacques Ellul's *The Technological Bluff*.[2]

This present concern about the legitimate role of individuals is not the old Western preoccupation with individualism. Nor is

110

it the 1960s youth culture concern with freedom.[3] The impulse is very different. While the focus of the counter culture youth movements was freedom *from* the constraints and false values of the consumer society, the present emphasis is freedom *for* responsibility. Simply put, the focus is that people become fully human when they assume responsibility for the life they live and the choices they make. Keeping people dependent undermines their full humanity.

These various emphases in philosophy, education and community work with their particular nuances can be subsumed under a specific theme. It is this: How can people be empowered to responsibly assume greater control over their own lives and thereby become less dependent on external controls and on the guardianship of experts?

This theme is neither utopian nor anarchistic. It does not envisage a world without structures and it does not call for the overthrow of particular systems. But it does call for their transformation. It envisages a growth process where the increasing attainment of the one (empowerment for responsibility) will require a corresponding decrease in the other (structures of guardianship). What this means regarding church, for example, is that to the degree that people assume responsibility for being *the* church, to that degree the reliance on organisational structures can be minimised.

Let me use an example from a non-church area to show how this works. When people with disabilities are moved out of institutionalised settings based on the medical model of care and control and are trained for community living, they will be able to assume greater responsibility for their lives. This is not the old libertinism, with its dream of freedom *from* responsibility. It is precisely the opposite: a vision of freedom *for* responsibility.

When we take this motif to Scripture with its corresponding questions, we are pleasantly surprised. Scripture also knows something about people empowerment and a breaking free from dependence on structures and systems. As we shall see, this has implications for the way we practise church.

THE BIBLE AND PEOPLE EMPOWERMENT

In this section I will lay a framework for beginning a theology of this new insight of people empowerment by drawing together a number of themes in Scripture. This in no way makes a claim to be exhaustive.

Control is replaced by radical freedom in Christ

The integration point for the theme of people empowerment is the Pauline assertion that we are no longer "subject to guardians and trustees," nor to the "basic principles of the world," for in Christ Jesus we have received our inheritance as sons and daughters of God (Galatians 4, verses 1 to 7).

Paul's powerful summary statement requires some unpacking. Not only does Paul see us as living beyond the legalism of the Old Testament law, but he also sees us as no longer subject to the fallen structures and systems of this world.

This does mean that the Christian freed by the power of Christ rejects the moral principles of the Old Testament. It simply means that the Christian transcends them. Christians not only do not kill their neighbours, but are motivated to love their enemies (Romans 12, verse 20). Such a radical morality is beyond systems and structures. This cannot be legislated. But it can be lived by the person who has linked radical freedom to loving responsibility and service.

Moreover, this does not mean that the Christian becomes a lawless member of society. The Christian is always the citizen of two communities: the community of faith and the socio-political order of the country to which he or she belongs. But the values of the former take priority over those of the latter. The Christian essentially is a change agent. To put that more radically, the Christian in essence is a subversive. The Christian as an agent of salt and light seeks to transform the socio-political order that it may conform more fully to the values of the kingdom of God. To live like that means to live beyond the ultimacy of the present structures and systems. It is this concept of radical freedom in Christ (Galatians 5, verse 1) which undergirds the notion of people empowerment and which has given Christianity its potentially life-changing and societal transforming message.

However, the theme of people empowerment need not only be built on a selection of passages from the New Testament. The Old Testament is also most instructive.

While there are many possible points of departure in the Old Testament for developing this theological theme, the most basic is Israel's disastrous experience of kingship. This is a classic example of a guardian structure gone horribly wrong. The premonarchic tribal confederacy, with people coming together in times of crisis under the temporary leadership of a Spirit-endowed person, was regarded by Israel as insufficient and ineffective. Israel wanted a king like the other nations (Deuteronomy 17, verses 14 to 20).

In spite of the careful checks and balances so that the king would not become a law unto himself but would remain subject to God's law (Deuteronomy 17, verse 19), and Samuel's warnings, Israel persisted in its walk towards the monarchy.

Samuel in 1 Samuel 8, verses 11 to 18 could not have spelt out more clearly the fatal consequences:

> This is what the king who will reign over you will do. He will take your sons and make them serve with his chariots and horses, and they will run in front of his chariots. Some he will assign to be commanders of thousands and commanders of fifties, and others to plough his ground and reap his harvest,

and still others to make weapons of war and equipment for his chariots. He will take your daughters to be perfumers and cooks and bakers. He will take the best of your fields and vineyards and olive groves and give them to his attendants. He will take a tenth of your grain and of your vintage and give it to his officials and attendants. Your menservants and maidservants and the best of your cattle and donkeys he will take for his own use. He will take a tenth of your flocks, and you yourselves will become his slaves. When that day comes, you will cry out for relief from the king you have chosen, and the Lord will not answer you in that day.

Not only did Israel not listen to these warnings, but subsequent societies—as Max Weber has noted—have walked a similar road. The movement has been towards greater organisational controls, greater government intervention and the development of a technological elite.[4]

Israel's march towards the monarchy not only destroyed the far greater people participatory structure under the old tribal system (Deuteronomy 1, verses 15 to 18), but also developed class distinctions and the gap between rich and poor, which became the focus of the prophetic critique (Isaiah 10, verses 1 to 4 and Amos 5, verses 7 to 27).

As Conrad Boerma has clearly pointed out, the monarchy did not simply mean a new political structure. It also created a new social reality. For with the kingship there developed a whole new mercantile elite and, in time, the radical egalitarianism based on tribal and family land was undermined. Elitism led to exploitation and injustice. This became the focus of the prophetic call to repentance[5]

While there were exceptions (2 Kings 14, verse 3), the pathetic refrain which captures the heart of Israel's experience of kingship was that the king "committed all the sins his father

114

had done before him" (1 Kings 15:3). Although the kingly ideal was to serve the people with justice (Proverbs 29, verse 14), the reality was that justice only came from the Lord (Proverbs 29, verse 26).

As a result of this major failure in guardianship—where the structure of kingly rule led to the abuse of power and kings led the people astray, thus abusing their sacred trust as shepherds of God's people—the prophets began to look towards a very different future. The vision for the permanence of the Davidic rule was transmuted into the vision of the servant role of the coming Messiah (Isaiah 42, verses 1 to 7).

In other words, the prophetic vision for the future was *not* a reconstructed kingship. This guardian structure had failed totally. The vision instead was the transformation that would occur through the coming of Isaiah's suffering servant. The hope in the old rulership was replaced by themes of redemption and deliverance (Isaiah 53, verses 1 to 12; Isaiah 61, verses 1 to 6). The future hope was centred in a transformed people who had been forgiven and healed and upon whom the Spirit rested rather than in new structures.

Moreover, a vision emerged which would see the replacement of institutionalised forms of power, expressed in the roles of priest and king. A day was coming when all God's people would be empowered by the Spirit and not only Israel's guardians (Joel 2, verses 28 and 29).

While the Old Testament contains its own internal critique of kingly rule, the New Testament mounts a critique of the other guardian structure: the priesthood and the law. Paul's criticism of guardianship in Galatians 5, verses 1 to 18 particularly focuses on the law and its inability to provide salvation and true freedom.

But Paul's critique goes further than simply the rejection of priestly guardianship. He mounts a radical critique on all systems and structures that keep people in bondage. He speaks of people being "in slavery under the basic principles of the world" (Galatians 4, verse 3). While he recognises that all authorities, systems and structures "in heaven and on earth" were initially created good by Christ (Colossians 1, verse 15), they were subject to the Fall. Thus all forms of human rulership, ideology and structure were infected by the distorting reality of human sinfulness.

As Jacques Ellul points out, the Fall did not only affect individuals.[6] It also affected the world itself which, being subject to "bondage and decay," now awaits "the glorious freedom of the children of God" (Romans 8, verses 20 and 21). Moreover, the Fall affected all the human systems that we create, including our economic and political systems. These very systems claim to guard and protect us. But so often the very systems that are meant to serve us exploit us instead. While the distorting power of Fascism or Communism readily springs to mind, we should not be blind to the more subtle perversions that more readily accepted ideologies and institutions promulgate. We need only think of the double justice that exists in the Western world— acquittal for the rich and incrimination for the poor.

We humans are so adept at creating our own philosophies, systems and institutions and these carry such promise for good but, in the final analysis, they fail to deliver and are in fact a charade. Their ineptitude and their well-camouflaged, evil intent is nowhere better demonstrated than when the priestly guardians of Jerusalem joined forces with the Roman political system to do away with God's demonstration of what the new humanity should be like in the person of Jesus Christ. Therefore, Paul can boldly declare that Christ, "having disarmed the powers and authorities. . . made a public spectacle of them, triumphing over them by the cross" (Colossians 2, verse 15).

Allow me to put that differently. If ever there was a time when the guardianship of priest and politician failed in their sacred duty towards the people for whom they were responsible, it was when they crucified God's Son. They attempted to do away with the very one who came to bring new life and a whole new ethic for living.

It follows that while Christians should not withdraw from the world but be actively involved in its transformation, they should nevertheless have a healthy, critical attitude towards all social systems and institutions which claim to help the people, but so frequently merely help themselves. The failure of the guardianship of the Old Testament kings, then, in some ways symbolises the failure of the guardianship of subsequent structures be they political, economic or religious.

Structures are replaced by interpersonal relationships

Rejecting both the political and the religious guardianship, the New Testament forges a new social order where structures are replaced by interpersonal relationships based on a common faith relationship in Christ Jesus. This new relationship not only explodes the old racial and cultural boundaries along with economic and gender discriminations, but also creates a community of mutual care, encouragement and economic sharing (Romans 15, verses 1 to 6 and 2 Corinthians 8, verses 13 to 15). Moreover, this life together in Christ Jesus is essentially anti-institutional.

While one could resort to unhelpful sloganeering such as "Jesus was concerned about the kingdom of God, early Christianity was concerned about the church" or "Jesus started a movement, Paul founded an institution," this does not help us all that much. What is more helpful is to recognise that the early Christian communities of the first century AD were quite unlike the contemporary institutions we call church. They were

117

much more like fellowship groups that met in people's homes. Put simply, the early Christian communities were much more a brotherhood and sisterhood centred in the person of Jesus Christ than an institutional reality.

Furthermore, the New Testament makes no attempt to spell out the structural, economic and social implications of this new Jesus movement. It develops no specific political theories, establishes no platform for major social and economic change, and fails to give specific contours for its own community life despite the fact that we can see several models of church in outline such as the Jerusalem community and the Pauline house churches. But there is little attempt to spell out the formal and structural implications of a particular model.

It seems as if the New Testament is primarily interested in the new relationship in Christ and the way Christians are to share life together. Hence, there is an emphasis on love, care, encouragement, support, sharing and service rather than on the formal structures of what it means to be church. In fact, the stance of the people of the early Christian communities is more eschatalogical than programmatic, calling people to live in the world but not dominated by it, "for this world in its present form is passing away" (1 Corinthians 7, verses 29 to 31).

This does not mean that the Christian is unconcerned about the state of the world. It does mean that the world does not set the agenda. The Christian lives by the divine contrariness of Jesus. This includes a scepticism about the structures and systems of the world.

In the light of the above, it is necessary to part company with pre-Vatican II thinking in the Roman Catholic Church and Reformation theology of church. Both, in various ways, have opted for an optimism regarding the guardianship model.

During the Middle Ages, the kingly and priestly modes of protecting society in the name of God were brought into collusion. Church and state were in a holy alliance and the twin pillars of society were the Bible and the sword. Far from being a counter-community, the church was at times the ruler of the nations and at other times the handmaiden of the state.

Everything about this period was by no means wholly negative. The church at least had to develop a theology and ethic that embraced the whole of society.[7] The church of that time could hardly be well served by a narrow theology and an ethic that was overly preoccupied with personal morality and had no vision for social morality. But the church at that time failed to establish a vision that empowered the people. Instead, it developed the power and control of the church's hierarchy and fortified the institutional aspect of the church's life.

The Reformation churches did little better. Luther joined forces with the German princes to form a state church. And Calvin so emphasised the role of the state that he held that the magistrate's task was a special calling of God similar to that of the pastor.[8] The Reformation churches also emphasised the institutional nature and role of the church and promoted the task of Christians to "manage" society in the name of Christian values. In a country such as The Netherlands, the Reformed churches promoted the role of Christian schools to train people for their role in the world and the formation of Christian political parties to "rule" society in the light of God's word.

While contemporary Roman Catholic and Reformation churches are far less optimistic about their rulership role (although the modern-day reconstructionists maintain this optimism), in a pluralistic age where the church, particularly in the West, has become a minority, the church has nevertheless maintained its subservience of the individual's need to that of the institution. People fit into the church's structures, programs and priorities. In no way can the people of God themselves create more appropriate structures, programs and priorities.

Not only is the idea of guardianship unwarranted in the light of Scripture, but it fails to provide an adequate analysis of the nature of structural evil that permeates the systems that we create—including our ecclesiastical systems.

Let me come at this summary statement somewhat differently. While the Old Testament itself signals the failure of the kingship and the priesthood, the New Testament does not promote a new guardianship. Instead, it promotes a new brotherhood and sisterhood with an emphasis on relationships rather than a particular institutional structure.

But even more significantly, the New Testament mounts a critique of the structures we create through the doctrine of the fallen powers (Ephesians 6, verse 12 and Colossians 2, verses 13 to 15). These fallen powers are not simply fallen angels or demons. They also have to do with the fallenness of our ideologies and the political and social institutions that we create. This includes our religious systems.[9]

The present optimism about the highly structured nature of the church with its secular management principles fails to recognise the reality of institutional "violence." What I mean by this is that institutions create particular structures and a culture that is premised on self-perpetuation and self-maintenance and which readily discourages dissent and possible change. As a result, people are marginalised and "sacrificed" so that the institution may survive.

A far closer approximation to the New Testament picture of church than the "guardianship" model of the Roman Catholic and Reformation churches which seek to "manage" society is the Anabaptist model of the church as a counter-community.

Without wishing to idealise the Anabaptists, we can nevertheless learn from them. They thoroughly rejected the guardianship model. The church is not to rule society. It is to be a servant instead. As a consequence of this view, they argued for

120

the separation of church and state. Moreover, they stressed the communal nature of church rather than its institutional reality (see Leonard Verduin).[10]

Church as the responsibility of the few is replaced by church as the responsibility of all

This has significant implications for the way we understand church. We have identified in the New Testament an anti-structural and anti-institutional motif due to the fallen nature of the authorities and powers. We have also noted that early Christianity, rather than replacing its rejection of the priestly guardianship with an institutional model of its own, opted for an interpersonal focus based on sharing a common life in Christ. Thus redemption in Christ does not redeem the old guardianship, but calls for new ways of social existence.

Within the New Testament (excluding the pastoral epistles, which already reflect an emphasis on institutionalisation which was to become characteristic of the second and third centuries), there are many sub-themes that reinforce this thesis. Rather than guardianship, with its implicit idea that a stronger, wiser, more mature person needs to guard and direct our lives, the New Testament celebrates the notion of people empowerment. People with a new sense of identity because of their experience of Christ's salvation are brought into a common fraternity based on caring and sharing relationships, taking responsibility for their own lives and for their desire to be the transformative agents in the world.

As a consequence, the New Testament stresses that all have been empowered and gifted by the Spirit and all have a part to play in the body of Christ (1 Corinthians 12 to 14 and Romans 12).

1 Corinthians 12 emphasises that "to each one the manifestation of the Spirit is given for the common good"

121

(verse 7) and Paul goes on to point out that "the body is not made up of one part but of many" (verse 14). Further, unlike other social institutions which are characterised by hierarchical structures or social differentiation, the church is to be different in that "God has combined the members of the body and given greater honour to the parts that lacked it, so that there should be no division in the body, but that its parts should have equal concern for each other" (verses 24 and 25).

Moreover, roles and functions in the early church are emphasised rather than offices and position. Paul highlights in Romans 12, verses 4 to 8 that:

> Just as each of us has one body with many members, and these members do not all have the same function, so in Christ we who are many form one body and each member belongs to all the others. We have different gifts, according to the grace given us. If a man's gift is prophesying, let him use it in proportion to his faith. If it is serving, let him serve; if it is teaching, let him teach; if it is encouraging, let him encourage; if it is contributing to the needs of others, let him give generously; if it is leadership, let him govern diligently; if it is showing mercy, let him do it cheerfully.

Church structures are not spelled out in the New Testament, but caring relationships are. Everywhere in the Pauline epistles is the call to love, serve, care and support each other (Romans 14, verse 19; chapter 15, verse 7; Galatians 6, verse 2; chapter 6, verse 10; Ephesians 5, verse 21; Colossians 3, verses 12 to 17). Power relationships are deliberately transmuted into servanthood priorities. In Mark 10, verses 42 to 43, we read Jesus' words:

> You know that those who are regarded as rulers of the Gentiles lord it over them and their high officials exercise author-

ity over them. Not so with you. Instead, whoever wants to become great among you must be your servant and whoever wants to be first must be slave of all. For even the Son of Man did not come to be served, but to serve and to give his life as a ransom for many.

Finally, no ecclesiastical structures are created, but familial relationships are emphasised (Acts 2, verse 46 and Acts 16, verse 15). This particularly comes to the fore in the New Testament's emphasis on the church as the "body of Christ" and the "household of faith."

This means that neither priest with altar, nor preacher with pulpit are intrinsic to the New Testament vision of the church as body of Christ. This is a radical realisation. Not only is the modern notion of a full-time professional minister alien to the spirit of the New Testament, but the modern institutionalised version of church is a parody of the life together that the New Testament envisages. Christians can meet at any time in any place for the purposes of listening to Scripture, prayer, worship, mutual help and encouragement, breaking bread, baptism and mission with a functional rather than positional leadership.

In other words, the church of the New Testament is much more a family than an institution. And the primary reason why this is significant for us today is because many institutions operate on the guardianship model. That is, they control and determine for people the goods and services that are meant to be good for them. But they don't put *real* power and responsibility in their hands.

This radically de-institutionalised form of being together, with each one playing their part, places the responsibility for being church into the hands of all the people of God. It is the mutual sharing of this responsibility that will empower God's people for growth and mission, since the reliance on the guardian, the cleric, the expert and the structures that so conveniently carry us along has been taken away.

In this chapter, I have brought the contemporary question of people empowerment to Scripture. This is not the only pressing question that relates to the nature of the church, but it is an important one. I have not sought to set out a step-by-step exegetical picture of people empowerment as a key motif for understanding the church; this would have made the book far too large and filled it with specialist jargon. But the issue of people empowerment which has become a more and more pressing issue today is a matter that is not unknown to Scripture. In fact, people empowerment is a biblical motif, given the criticism of the guardianship model and the emphasis on people being the body of Christ.

The next step is to explore some of the practical implications of this alternative understanding of being church and to suggest ways in which it can be made achievable.

ENDNOTES

1. Thomas S. Kuhn, *The Structure of Scientific Revolutions*, University of Chicago, 1962

2. Jacques Ellul, *The Technological Bluff*, Eerdmans, 1990

3. See Theodore Roszak, *The Making of a Counter Culture*, Doubleday, 1969.

4. See Max Weber: *On Charisma and Institution Building*, S.N. Eisenstadt (ed.), University of Chicago, 1968.

5. Conrad Boerma, *The Rich, the Poor and the Bible*, Westminster, 1978

6. Jacques Ellul, *The Ethics of Freedom*, Eerdmans, 1976

7. See Jacques Ellul, *The New Demons*, Seabury, 1975.

8. See Willem Balke, *Calvin and the Anabaptist Radicals,* Eerdmans, 1981.

9. Walter Wink, *Unmasking the Powers: The Invisible Forces that Determine Existence,*, Fortress, 1986.

10. See Leonard Verduin, *The Reformers and their Stepchildren*, Eerdmans, 1964.

CHAPTER 8

THE VISION IN ACTION

How people empowerment can work

A good place to start considering the practical implications of the people empowerment model is to acknowledge that many Christians do *not* find themselves in a context where empowerment is easily achievable. Instead, they experience the more traditional ways of being church.

For many in our larger urban centres, this means driving many kilometres on Sunday to one's favourite large church. This church is usually program-dominated and the entire "ceremony" is carefully executed from the podium for the people's benefit and edification. The orientation is not too dissimilar to going to a concert, a public rally or a drama presentation, except that in church there is somewhat more participation, particularly in singing. The similarity between this type of church and a concert is that both are performance-based and people come to enjoy and benefit from the particular ceremony.

This way of being church—whether the focus is the eucharist, the liturgy, the sermon or charismatic worship—operates on the premise that a particular service is provided for the people by religious professionals. Those who attend contribute little to the overall ceremony and experience little solidarity with others who are there. While people can enter into the spirit of the performance, they themselves do not contribute significantly to what happens in church on that particular Sunday. They are more spectators than participants. Church happens to them by means of a ceremony; they are not practising being church themselves.

The related difficulty with performance-based events is that people come for the event and then disperse. There is little opportunity for connecting up with each other at a meaningful level. Put in its worst light, this is a cafeteria style of Christianity where you quickly get your "spiritual" food and then go home.

Attempts to make up for this lack of solidarity among churchgoers by the formation of midweek cell or pastoral care groups is an acknowledgment of the problem. But this hardly provides a significant overall solution.

This approach often fails for several reasons. First, only some church members belong to the midweek group. Second, this meeting is often a mini-church service. Third, the dominant reality still is what happens on Sundays.

A minority of Christians, however, experience church quite differently—as members of intentional communities, base ecclesial communities and house churches. While these alternative ways of being church have different forms, they share a common ethos. Key to this ethos is the ideal that the people *are* the church and have responsibility for its shape, life and mission. The people actually make the decisions and are responsible for their outworking. We shall now look at these three models of church in turn. (It should be borne in mind, however, as we do so that there are many other alternative church models that there is no room to treat here. The community church movement, for instance, has many people empowering characteristics.)

Intentional Christian community usually refers to people who have contracted or covenanted to share a common way of life and common objectives and who live together in some form of shared lifestyle.[1] A group that immediately springs to mind is the Amish in Pennsylvania, USA, made popular in the dramatic movie *Witness*. A similar group with an Anabaptist ethos is the Bruderhof, also in the USA.[2] But there are also many contemporary examples of Christian intentional community.

In the 1970s, Post Green and the Community of Celebration were well-known communities in Britain. Reba Place Fellowship, among many others, became popular in the USA around the same time.[3] Equally well-known in the USA are the Catholic charismatic covenant communities.[4] And in Australia, The House of the Gentle Bunyip and The House of Freedom readily spring to mind as examples of this form of community.[5]

The base ecclesial communities are different in form to that of the intentional communities. They are less structured and in some ways function more like what we popularly understand by small fellowship groups. But they are different from fellowship groups in that they have a much greater emphasis on solidarity and common ministry. While the base ecclesial communities are usually associated with the emergence of the church of the poor in Latin America, they have, in fact, sprung up all over the world.[6]

The base ecclesial communities are more practically described as consisting of ten to thirty persons who share a common faith in Christ, who relate deeply to one another in the form of spiritual and practical care and who seek together to minister to their neighbourhood.[7] They are more theoretically described as a new and original way of being church which is gathered around word and sacrament and which focuses on the ministries of lay people. Such communities utilise participatory processes, and decisions for their life and ministry are made by the people themselves.[8]

For many members in the Catholic base ecclesial communities, involvement in these communities is based on a dual experience: on the one hand, they still relate to the church as an institutional, sacramental and priestly reality; on the other hand, they experience church as people in solidarity with each other and in their particular neighbourhoods.[9] By contrast, where Protestants are involved in intentional communities, base ecclesial communities or house churches, these tend to be their sole and distinct way of being church.

There are undoubtedly multiple reasons for this difference between Roman Catholics and Protestants. One is that the Catholic Church has traditionally been structured on diversity while retaining a hierarchical and sacramental centre. Protestants, on the other hand, base church on a uniform reality and consequently have adopted the splinter principle.

This is possibly a reason why many (though not all) in the house church movement in Australia come out of a Protestant background. For them, the house church is their only way of being church. This way of being church has many similarities to the base ecclesial communities. However, house churches are more a middle-class Western phenomenon, while the base ecclesial communities are more prevalent among the Third World's poor.

Key concepts of the house church are: church as family, sharing all of life and not simply the spiritual aspects, the key role of the laity, and the sharing of gifts and ministries that will build up all the members for their growth in Christian maturity and for their service in the world.[10]

Clearly, these three alternative ways of being church— intentional community, base ecclesial community and house church—more closely approximate the people empowerment model than the more traditional ways. But they are not necessarily the same as the model suggested here. They are similar when they emphasise solidarity expressed in a life of practical caring and sharing and when people are empowered for responsibility. But they are dissimilar when they remain expert-led or emphasise their particular structure as *the* way of being church.

Let me explain this. Some intentional Christian communities have developed rather authoritarian leadership structures. A related observation is that people join particular forms of Christian community for emotional security and fail to grow into maturity and responsibility. Instead, they remain vulnerable and dependent.

Also, some alternative forms of being church are being promoted as the way in which we express our being the people of God. This development is most unfortunate. The practical implication of this kind of thinking is that if you don't structure your corporate way of expressing the Christian life in a particular way, you are in fact living at some sub-standard level. While not going quite so far, T. J. Saxby[11] nevertheless moves in that direction with his emphasis on shared possessions as a key element in being church.

The people empowerment model, on the other hand, focuses on certain processes and allows for many *forms* of being church. It particularly maintains that no ultimacy can be given to any single form. The reason for this is that processes are more important than structures. In other words, the issue is not so much that we find an ideal form of church. The focus instead is that people are empowered to be responsible and find their own appropriate ways of expressing their life together.

Some key elements in the New Testament view of church are: people need to be in relationship to Christ and in solidarity with each other, serving God, each other and the world in any and every way that does not undermine peoplehood. The people empowerment model stresses that growth in Christ and in our spirituality, as well as in our humanity, is keenly related to being treated as responsible sons and daughters of God and not as children under the sway of guardians.

Thus this model rejects the notion that house church is *the* New Testament way of being church. It is simply one possible model among many others. It also rejects the idea of communities continuing to be led by experts and structured more for safety from the big bad world than for responsibility towards it. Such "safe" structures produce immaturity rather than empowerment. The idea of joining Christian community in order to feel safe and secure may well mean that community becomes another guardian structure. The community thus makes decisions for me, the community gives meaning to my life and the community orders my life direction and its priorities. Clearly, this results in dependence rather than empowerment.

Given, then, that most Christians experience traditional church rather than community or house church, how can they move towards this new model? And how can those who are in alternative ways of being church that become disempowering for them benefit from this approach?

It would be foolish in the extreme not to recognise that any number of factors must come together for people to begin to move towards the new model. Many people simply accept the traditional model of being church as self-evident and as God-ordained, when in fact they should recognise that we play a part in shaping the human face of the church. Moreover, one can hardly expect traditional clergy to teach doctrines that undermine their own position. And when all is said and done, traditional church is most convenient. Simply put, our modern world with its supermarkets has helped to shape us into thinking that a supermarket Christianity is appropriate for us.

However, in spite of these realities, the journey should be made in probing the factors that will move us to a more authentic way of being the people of God. In the rest of this chapter, I shall suggest ways to put this vision into action.

DARE TO QUESTION AND EXPLORE

People usually do not look to change the things with which they are familiar and comfortable. We seem to prefer continuity to change.

As a starting point, if things are to change, then something needs to occur in people's lives that will begin to cause a fissure in the smooth flow of tradition. The experience of alienation or frustration, the search for better ways, reading about past radical movements in church history, probing Scripture for new answers—these and many other catalysts can be used by the Holy Spirit to begin the painful search. What I am suggesting is that change becomes a possibility when the familiar is no longer credible. The old opinions are no longer satisfactory, so we begin to look at things in a new way by exploring new questions and options.

Unfortunately, many people's search for the new ends precisely here. For they wrongly assume that questioning tradition automatically brings alternatives into being. They are usually badly mistaken. Genuinely new answers and approaches do not come that easily. And it is much harder to shake off the old than what we may think. Since the old has become a part of our present value system and is therefore a part of our understanding, the old is usually far more tenacious and persistent. Peter Berger's thesis is that we move from the process of externalisation (by the outpouring of human mental and physical activity into the world) to objectification (by the creation of particular products, systems and programs). We then internalise the things we have made to the point that they form our subjective consciousness so that we assume that this is now the way things are meant to be.[12] If this thesis of externalisation-objectification-internalisation is correct, then radical change is indeed difficult.

I am not only suggesting that significant change is difficult. I am also suggesting that to question the old does not necessarily lead smoothly to the discovery of the new. Instead, the search for the new may be an invitation to being misunderstood, further alienated and becoming a candidate for the experience of pain. Not only must this experience of pain be recognised quickly lest one sinks into the quagmire of anger and reaction, but one needs to move forward by joining with others in the common search for alternatives. There are usually some other people who have begun the journey in a similar direction.

Let me illustrate what I mean by this. If a person becomes a religious refugee because the church was resistant to change at some critical point, then that hardly means that this person has all the answers. Furthermore, if such a person remains a solitary in the place of alienation, he or she may well become even less a source of wisdom for discerning and building the new. In other words, people who are marginalised and hurt can barely save themselves. They are not well placed to be of much help to formulate a new vision.

It is imperative, therefore, to deal not only with hurt and rejection, but also to find a counter-community, a group of people who are also struggling with bringing the new into being. Together, exploration of new ways of being church can take place.

This exploratory phase must be kept open for a longer rather than a shorter period of time. It is very human to foreclose on this phase as quickly as possible. We all tend to be in a hurry to come to a new certainty and a new security. That is why, hot on the heels of the change agents, the bureaucrats are ready to move in. While there are probably many and varied explanations as to why this occurs, Emile Durkheim is insightful with his suggestion that the human being cannot cope with an extended period of anomie. We need our world to be predictable and taken for granted.[3]

This phase calls for the ability to live with ambiguity—having rejected aspects of the old, but with the new still in process of formulation, one literally lives in an in-between state. Moreover, one needs to give ample time for the old ways to be worked out of one's system. When this time is not taken, we tend to act out the old ways within a new structure. The consequence is that nothing much has really changed.

A good illustration of this phenomenon is what has taken place in much of charismatic renewal. It promised to change the face of the church. Instead, it has maintained the old structures, hierarchies and priorities. It has fostered the same old dependence, leaving the laity unempowered in terms of carrying the responsibility for being church and being God's agents of hope and change in the world.

In fact, charismatic renewal has so emphasised the role of the clergy that they have virtually been reinstated to a priestly role. This is not seen in terms of the altar, but in terms of intermediary spokespersons between God and humankind. It is ironic that a church renewal movement which so emphasised the availability of the power and gifts of the Spirit for each individual has managed to leave its members so marginalised in terms of responsibility. Here, the old has simply reasserted itself in spite of the promise of the new. It is an historical observation that the early emphasis in charismatic renewal on unity was soon supplanted by an emphasis on submission to the local church leadership. The former emphasis was simply too uncontrollable.

This danger of reproducing the old in the new must be resisted. While over time some things can be brought to closure, they may later need to be opened again. Thus the need for exploration remains continually with us. What I am suggesting is that empowerment begins when we dare to question the old and explore new possibilities. While questioning the old is the work of deconstruction, exploring the new is the work of reconstruction.

I have already pointed out that the work of reconstruction can come from a critical rereading of the Bible in the light of contemporary reality. I am now adding to this the practical observation that we also learn from putting ideas into practice. With mutual travellers, we reflect not only on Scripture and the lessons from the church's long two thousand years of history, but we also learn by doing. And when our practice involves exploration, we can over time fine-tune the things we are learning.

BE PREPARED TO BUILD THE NEW

There may be ideal circumstances in which this process of working towards a new model of being church can take place. One such context is where clergy and members in a traditional church structure share the same vision for change.

The idea that you cannot change the institutional church is clearly false. But the proposition that changing traditional church structures is difficult is clearly correct. An illustration of the difficulty is told in Athol Gill's *The Fringes of Freedom*.[4] A popular illustration of the possibility of change is Michael

Harper's account of the Church of the Redeemer in Houston, USA.[5]

While I do not wish to refer to one example of negotiated change between clergy and laity, I do wish to sketch out a composite profile of possibilities. In such a scenario, members can be trained to take greater responsibility for the life and mission of the church and the clergy can correspondingly take on depowered and changed roles.

What does this mean practically? First of all, decision-making becomes participatory. The people become responsible for the life, direction and mission of the church. Second, the people are trained to take on many of the roles usually taken by clergy. People can learn how to counsel, preach and do administrative tasks. Third, if more is done by the people, then the clergy can act more as resource persons and focus on training people.

The result will not only be a stronger laity, but also different types of worship services and different ministry priorities can emerge. Since no one person is the one who does it all and makes all the decisions, the work of being church—mutual care and service to the world—becomes a matter of pooling resources, time and skills on the part of all. Furthermore, worship times can take on more of a familial character. The worship service is no longer a carefully orchestrated ceremony. It is people meeting together to share their life of work, family, service, learning, struggle, hope and faith in the presence of God and in the light of Scripture.

This scenario does not mean that there is no longer a role for theologically trained persons. Quite the opposite is the case. Such persons can contribute their skills and knowledge, but they take their place alongside others who exercise other skills. The theologically trained person cannot, in most cases, be the amazing all-rounder anyway. Since when is one person a good teacher, preacher, organiser, visionary, comforter, counsellor and trainer? The theologian must take his or her place among God's people who must be mobilised to use the gifts God has given them.

What all this means is that there is no longer a place for the clergyperson who does all the preaching, celebration of the sacraments, organising, pastoral work and the hundred and one other tasks that keep the ecclesiastical system operating.

At another level, what the above means is that the church should adopt deinstitutionalisation processes. The organisational machinery should be streamlined and kept to a minimum. Particular roles should be diffused. Tasks should be shared. And familial nature rather than the institutional aspects of church should become the dominant reality.

Unfortunately, most of us live in the less than ideal circumstances where church leaders and people don't work together for change. What do we do then? Do we simply tolerate the present system? Do we drop out, frustrated and disillusioned? Or foolishly, as some have done, do we throw the baby out with the bathwater by denying the reality of our faith because of frustration with the ecclesiastical structure?

The answer is that we must start building the new. But we can only do this if we can ideologically depower the traditional church system. In other words, we need to overcome the idea that the present church alone is legitimate and that anything we do as an alternative is illegitimate. If we cannot overcome this hurdle, then we are beaten before we start. If we cannot change the system and we may not create the new, then we are banished to the realms of frustration and immobility. This seems to be the place to which many churchgoers have come. These people are unhappy with the way things are. They are afraid to create alternatives.

Yet much of church history is the journey of new beginnings, particularly since the Reformation. The Reformation churches

138

themselves, Wesleyanism, Pentecostalism and many other denominational groups, all came from new beginnings. Over time they have gained legitimacy and permanence. But their beginnings were probably no less fragile and small than the beginnings you and I need to make. When we think of the Reformed churches, the Anglican Church or the Assemblies of God, we think of them as inviolate realities. Yet they all had fragile beginnings—and so will be our attempt to shape a new way of being church.

The attempt to build a new way of being church cannot be a uniform endeavour. Different approaches and strategies will be necessary.

One approach that we have already considered is the ideal situation where clergy and laity can work in partnership to bring about change. But many other possibilities exist.

Another approach is what is occurring in Latin America. There, the Catholic base ecclesial communities are building the new *alongside* the old on the basis of complementarity. What this means is that the institutional church is maintained to perform its particular functions and the base communities are created to complement the institutional church. Thus in the base communities, people gather for fellowship, Bible study, prayer and caring help, and to plan ways to make an impact on their neighbourhoods. In the institutional church, they partake of the sacraments, are married, buried and receive further institutional services such as schools and hospitals. From the institutional church, they also receive doctrinal direction and help regarding socio-political issues.

The Catholic charismatic covenant communities in the West, while different in organisational structure to the base ecclesial communities, also exist alongside the institutional church on the basis of partnership. However, in these covenant communities the real life together, training in spiritual formation and works of service take place in the communities.

Others are building the new *underneath* the old. With friends and interested others they have begun to meet in their homes to share life together, pray, listen to Scripture and share in common strategies to affect their world. In the meantime, they continue to relate to the traditional church. However, the primary reality is often the regular but more informal getting together. This is where the real spiritual and other needs are met. The continuance in the formal church is usually out of a sense of duty or a desire not to rock the boat too much.

This is not unlike the Pietist experiment with its idea of "church within church." This approach allows for ongoing dialogue between the old and the new. The dialogue usually ends when the new group dares to take to itself the right to administer the sacraments.

Pietism emerged at the peak of Lutheran orthodoxy in Germany in the late seventeenth and early eighteenth centuries. The movement inspired by Philipp Spener sought to bring new life to formal Christianity. Spener instituted devotional circles for the purpose of prayer and Bible study in order that people might rediscover a heartfelt religion. Though he proclaimed the priesthood of all true believers, Spener did not encourage separation from the institutional church, but its transformation by a renewal from within. This Pietist option in bringing about church renewal and change is far from dead. It has continued to be an approach right up to the present.[6]

Others again begin to build the new by abandoning the old. Because of the particular difficulties of their situation, and because of hurt or antagonism, they cannot maintain a dialogue with the traditional church. They therefore need to forge the new in company with fellow travellers, but in isolation from the church which initially succoured them.

140

This is probably the most difficult of the various options that are open to us. This will require the ability to move beyond a purely reactive stance. Otherwise the old is merely condemned and the new never swims into view. If that hurdle can be successfully negotiated—and people can study the underside of church history by recovering the less dominant models, and can re-engage Scripture with new and pressing questions—then proactive possibilities can become dominant.

RECOGNISE THAT PEOPLE EMPOWERMENT IS NOT EASY

It is necessary at this point to lay to rest some possible misgivings on the part of some of my readers. I have already attempted, in previous chapters, to answer the question, "By what authority can these things be done?" But there are possibly other questions such as: Is the new not based on notions of libertinism? In other words, are the ideas expressed in this book not based on an extreme liberty of thought and action? And do these ideas of giving so much power and responsibility to "ordinary" people not undermine the very nature of church as we have traditionally understood it?

There are also other questions that the ideas of people empowerment give rise to. What about the issue of leadership? What about the need for specialised and gifted ministries so that the body of Christ can be built up? If the early church needed special people like the apostles, do we not need today highly gifted people to further lead the church, people that you would not find in your average house church or base ecclesial community? What about the need for institutionally-based ministries to the wider society that are a part of the traditional church? What about the need for church-based schools and hospitals and ministries of social welfare? And finally, one of the most nagging issues of all: Do not all renewal movements in time become institutionalised anyway? So why spend so much energy on reform?

All of these questions are important and I will return to them a little later. But they lead us straight to an indispensable observation: the people empowerment model is no picnic. The reason this new model is not easy is not only because it asks for greater involvement and responsibility, but because those who pursue it have to justify themselves over against the objections of the more traditional ways of being church.

Those who find traditional church hard should not attempt the new model in the hope that it will make life easier. The opposite is the case. If traditional church can be likened to a walk-in cafeteria, then the people empowerment model is where you learn not only to cook your own meals, but also to offer hospitality and feed the poor. Allow me to expand that a little further.

Traditional church is run by professionals and willing volunteers. The services church provides are laid on for you. In the new model, nothing is laid on. The people make everything happen. They run the worship services. They plan the program. They perform the ministry.

The people empowerment model, therefore, has nothing to do with the creation of little "bless-me" clubs where you meet with a few like-minded friends for some Christian fellowship because you are frustrated with the machinations of the institutional church. Such groups in the main stay reactive. Their focus is on what is wrong with the traditional model. But there is no vision for the new and no courage to begin to walk the difficult, but challenging road towards its realisation.

By contrast, the people empowerment model, as I have already stressed, is geared for responsibility. It seeks to place power in the hands of people so they become responsible under God for shaping their life together as Christians, for their *own* spiritual growth and development, and their *own* mission to the world. This means that the people decide how and when to meet and what are to be the processes for Christian growth and development. And they then are mobilised to make it happen.

The consequence of this is that they no longer come to church to get their weekly shot-in-the-arm or pep-talk. They come together for corporate fellowship as much to give as to receive. Consequently, singing may not only be corporate, but Bible study, sharing, prayer, holy communion and other activities of Christians meeting together may all involve far greater participation on the part of all present.

This giving rather than only receiving to people's lives is due to the fact that they have learnt for themselves the discipline of the spiritual life. Thus prayer, meditation and reflection on Scripture, worship and fasting are part of the rhythm of the spiritual life.[17]

What I am saying here is that people must begin to take responsibility for their own spiritual development. This is not at all to suggest that we are not spiritually enhanced by corporate worship, teaching and fellowship. Of course, we are. That is why it is so imperative that we come together as Christians in meaningful ways. But if I am merely relying on the group to stay spiritually afloat, I remain dependent and subject to guardianship.

Moreover, ministry and mission become part of one's personal as well as one's combined responsibility. Just as payment is no longer made for someone to do the clergy task because the people themselves perform such tasks, so one does not pay others to do ministry or mission on one's behalf. The challenge is to engage, where possible, in ministry oneself and in ministry together.

There is nothing *laissez-faire* about this way of being church. It is tough!

BE ASSURED THAT THE PEOPLE EMPOWERMENT
MODEL IS NOT ANARCHY

Here I need to return to some of the earlier questions and concerns that have been raised about this new model of church. This way of being church has nothing to do with libertinism, anarchy or looseness. It is not a place where anything goes. People are never empowered when they live dissipated lives or when they do "whatever, whenever they please." They are only empowered when they live disciplined, mutually accountable and mutually supportive lives.

When the people make the choices about the human face of the church, determine the nature of their life together and then assume responsibility for making it happen, this can hardly be anarchic. In fact, it is the opposite. It is living a disciplined life based on mutual accountability.

Moreover, this model is not anti-institutional. It instead favours *de*-institutionalisation, but it is not anarchic. The traditional image of church as institution is replaced by that of "people in relationships." This change in focus brings with it a particular organising principle all of its own. Replace the image of corporation with that of family and you have a very different social entity. But the latter does not necessarily spell chaos.

What I am simply saying is this: develop a corporation and you need certain organisational realities; develop a small business and you still need certain organisational realities—but not the same as that of a corporation. Similarly, if church is structured more like family rather than an institution, you still need certain organisational realities.

Put differently, if E.F. Schumacher can recommend an intermediate technology that has people in view, and not simply economic progress,[18] then similarly churches should be organised as if people mattered. In other words, the spiritual and social concerns of people should take priority over the needs of

144

church as institution. If churches are organised with people concerns at the centre, then the way such a church organises its life will of necessity be different. It will be structured in such a way that participatory processes are primary.[19]

Furthermore, this model maintains the importance of leadership. People empowerment places the issue of leadership into the hands of the group. They are responsible together for their corporate life and for their mission statement. To facilitate aspects of their life together, they may make use of rotating coordinators or facilitators. But leadership is no longer positionally-based or in the hands of a particular person, an arrangement which only tends to perpetuate the old guardianship model.

However, this is not to deny that certain people in the group may exercise informal leadership based on their greater life experience and wisdom. But their contributions should always be tested and affirmed by the group in order that the group may continue to own their corporate decisions.

Thus, the new model insists that neither natural abilities nor special charismatic gifts should become institutionalised. Similarily, elders do not need to have a positional role. They are simply those in the fellowship who have the gift of wisdom and the experience of life so that their advice and input can be happily received for discernment on the part of the group. Moreover, the new model acknowledges that the Holy Spirit has given gifts to all the members of the church. In the faithful exercise of these gifts (1 Corinthians 12; Romans 12) the church is built up and encouraged.

This sounds fine theoretically, but what does this mean practically? At the most basic level, it means that people need to discover the gifts and abilities that God has already given them. Hence, people need to be given opportunities tentatively to try a range of tasks. In time, certain ministry preferences will begin to emerge. While this process of discovery can be speeded up by programs that help people to discover their spiritual gifts[20] or their personality orientation through Myers-Briggs assessment,[21] it can also be allowed to take its own course.

Where people have the responsibility and opportunity to exercise a range of ministries, it becomes evident over time what people are particularly good at. They can then be encouraged to develop these abilities further through formal training if they so desire.

On the other hand, there is no place in the people empowerment model for the notion that if people have the gift of teaching they cannot learn other skills. In fact, the empowerment model operates on the idea that, in growing into maturity in Christ (Ephesians 4, verse 13), we must learn from our sisters and brothers in the faith and thereby open our horizons to new possibilities. There is nothing so stifling as dividing people into roles and functions rather than seeing them as creatures of God with significant potential for development.

People are basically not solo-gifted. A person is so much more than just a good administrator. A person cannot be categorised simply in terms of having a healing ministry. People are multi-gifted. They can do a range of things and should be encouraged to stretch beyond the familiar. This is at the heart of the empowerment model. If people are never given the opportunity to try certain new tasks, they come to believe that they can never do them.

I have so far responded to some of the questions of concern that I raised earlier. The new model has organisational reality, leadership and respects the contribution of gifted people.

One of the concerns that I still need to address is the role of institutionally-based ministries of the church such as schools, hospitals and social welfare ministries, since one local church will not be able to sustain such a large project.

There are two responses I would like to make. First, such ministries are still possible by churches working cooperatively and where such projects are put under the control of parent-based, community-based or parachurch-based organisations. There is no need to justify the maintenance of the institutional machinery of church by arguing for the validity of community services that are clearly worthwhile. Such services can be maintained in other ways.

The second point is that if the church de-institutionalises itself, new welfare and community services can emerge.

With no ecclesiastical institutions to upkeep let alone build, the new church is freed to place significant amounts of money into its service to the world. More importantly, it will no longer build institutionally-based human care services which reflect its own institutional self-understanding.

Because the traditional church has so thoroughly seen itself in institutional terms, it has provided many human care services built on that model. The new model of being church, on the other hand, has the opportunity to provide ministries based on a community or self-help model of human service provision. Since empowerment for growth and responsibility is the key motif for the church's life, this also becomes a key motif in its ministry strategy to others. In other words, if the church's self-understanding changes significantly away from institutional to more people participatory models, then the ministries and services the church provides will begin to reflect these newer values and models. Instead of building institutionally-based welfare services, the church is more likely to provide community-based services.

These then are some pointers in the development of the people empowerment model. In essence, I am saying that empowerment occurs in an amalgam of ways. First, people need a vision that new ways of being church are both desirable and possible. Second, people need to be freed from the tyranny of the old structures which keep people dependent. Third, people need to explore. They need to find the space and the companions on the road to experiment with new ways of being church. Fourth, such a new model of church needs to empower people by giving them responsibility for the group's life, structure, maintenance and ministry priorities.

These, then, are some practical implications in the outworking of the new vision of what it means to be the people of God. Some will possibly be frustrated that I have not spelt out the nuts and bolts of the new model. That, however, would defeat the purpose. The new model is based on processes, not on structures. These processes primarily have to do with encouraging and equipping each other to assume greater responsibility for our own lives, and for our spiritual growth and ministry to each other and the world. The model is based on the idea that we learn much by doing and we grow through assuming responsibility.

The long-term implications of the desire to walk this road are hardly in our hands. Hopefully, the end result will be an end to the supermarket Christianity, where everything is laid on for us and to which we have become so accustomed, and the emergence of a much more flexible, trim, self-disciplined and open-ended form of Christianity.

Should this eventually lead again to institutionalisation and rigidity, this can only indicate that the new has lost its way and needs to start again. In fact, the need to start again is what this book is all about, since change should be welcomed as a friend rather than seen as an enemy who seeks to disturb our slumber in the structures of guardianship.

ENDNOTES

1. See David Clark, *Basic Communities: Towards an Alternative Society*, SPCK, 1977.

2. See Benjamin Zablocki, *The Joyful Community*, Penguin, 1971.

3. See Donald G. Bloesch, *Wellsprings of Renewal: Promise in Christian Communal Life*, Eerdmans, 1974.

4. See Stephen B. Clark, *Patterns of Christian Community: A Statement of Community Order*, Servant, 1984.

5. See Athol Gill, *The Fringes of Freedom*, Lancer, 1990.

6. See M.&I. Fraser, *Wind and Fire*, Basic Communities Resource Centre, 1986.

7. See James O'Halloran, *Signs of Hope: Developing Small Christian Communities*, Orbis, 1991.

8. See Leonardo Boff, *Church: Charism and Power*, SCM, 1985.

9. See *The Challenge of Basic Christian Commmunities*, S. Torres & J. Eagleson (eds), Orbis, 1981.

10. See Robert & Julia Banks, *The Church Comes Home: A New Base for Community and Mission*, Albatross, 1989.

11. T.J. Saxby, *Pilgrims of A Common Life: Christian Community of Goods through the Centuries*, Herald, 1987

12. Peter Berger, *The Social Reality of Religion*, Penguin, 1967

13. See D. Ashley & D.M. Orenstein, *Sociological Theory: Classical Statements*, Allyn & Bacon, 1985.

14. Athol Gill, *The Fringes of Freedom*, Lancer, 1990

15. See Michael Harper, *A New Way of Living*, Logos, 1973.

16. For an interesting historical study on this approach, see F. Ernest Stoeffler, *Continental Pietism and Early American Christianity*, Eerdmans, 1976.

17. See the author's *Dare to Journey* with Henri Nouwen, Albatross, 1992.

18. E.F. Schumacher, *Small is Beautiful: Economics as if People Mattered*, Harper and Row, 1973.

19. See Lois Barrett, *Building the House Church*, Herald, 1986.

20. See James Clinton, *Spiritual Gits: A Self-Study and Group-Study*

Manual, Horizon House, 1985.

    21. See D. Keirsey and M. Bates, *Please Understand Me: Character and Temperament Types*, Prometheus Nemesis, 1984.

CHAPTER 9

A CHANGE OF LIFESTYLE

How Jesus can be made central

The discussion to this point has been on a rather serious note. This is hardly surprising. The issue of church for most Christians is a rather serious subject. After all, even though church may be a frustrating experience at times, we cannot abandon the concept of church. Church is God's idea. And even those who try to drive a wedge between Jesus and Paul with the idea that Jesus was concerned about the kingdom of God while Paul focussed on the church will have to admit that Jesus also created a community of disciples (Mark 3, verses 13 to 15 and Mark 9, verses 29 to 31).

Being the people of God, being community, being in solidarity is not some strange afterthought on the part of God. God is a community of persons as Father, Son and Holy Spirit and, as such, God is the great community-builder. God's concern has always been to create a people who will reflect in the world something of God's love, care and justice.[1]

Dietrich Bonhoeffer has clearly pointed out that the idea of a Christian as a solitary is unknown to the New Testament. Being a Christian is being called into *koinonia*.[2]

We recognise that being a Christian does not only mean being linked to Christ by faith, but also being part of the body of Christ, the community of faith (1 Corinthians 12, verses 12 and 13). Our baptism underscores this fact. In this sacrament, our link to Christ is affirmed (Romans 6, verses 3 and 4) and our being part of the Christian community is made visible. Similarly, in the celebration of the Lord's Supper, we celebrate both Christ's death for us and that he has called us into a common life. Nowhere is that put more clearly than by Paul: "And is not the bread that we break a participation in the body of Christ? Because there is one loaf we, who are many, are one body, for we all partake of the one loaf" (1 Corinthians 10, verses 16 and 17). Consequently, we can confess with the church of all ages and places that we believe "in the communion of the saints."

Church, therefore, can hardly be peripheral to our lives. In fact, it should be central. And because of its importance, we have grappled with its relevance in the pages of this book. The direction I have suggested involves a quantum leap. Instead of suggesting a facelift for the church, I have recommended a radical reconstruction. I do so because I see the church as basically an institutionally-driven entity which provides religious services for people, but fails to empower people for responsibility.

Little wonder that this has been "serious business"— particularly, since I am recommending that the very rules of the church as we know it be changed: that the bureaucratic aspects of church as institution be dispensed with and that, in its place, we see the emergence of groupings of people for fellowship and encouragement in which they themselves are responsible for their corporate life and ministry.

There's a new wind blowing past the walls of the old broken structures and we need to step out and catch it. But we need to be careful, lest we catch the wind, but sail in the wrong direction. The "wrong direction" is where the new way of being church becomes so central to our lives that the celebration of the messianic lifestyle and mission to which Jesus calls us becomes much too secondary. In other words, developing new models of church should not be our major preoccupation or become an end in itself. Church is the matrix in which we are sustained, built up and empowered in order to be light, salt and leaven in the world.

I want to come at this assertion from two different angles:

First, Christ, not the church, must be central

One's relationship with Christ through a continued obedient listening to his word and Spirit must remain the central reality of one's journey of faith. Church is one of the places where one expresses this walk of faith in solidarity with others, but it is not the only place. Christ must remain primary, the church secondary.

Let me put that another way. Christ is to be Lord of the whole of one's life. This means that we are to work out what his Lordship means in the family, the workplace, the broader structures of society and in the church. We cannot be solely preoccupied with Christ's Lordship in the church.

However, the assertion that Christ must be primary and the church must remain secondary is not an affirmation of Western individualism which is so rampant in the church. I am not promoting the old "God and me" mentality which celebrates the vertical relationship and minimises the horizontal. Instead, the assertion is a condemnation of "group-think" and social solidarity for its own sake.

Nor is the new model of church the replacement of one's vertical relationship with God by one's horizontal relationships with others. This will eventually only lead to an ugly uniformity which is debilitating rather than empowering. At the extreme lunatic fringe of this phenomenon, Jim Jones and his Temple of Doom and David Koresh and the tragedy at Waco, Texas, readily spring to mind. But in much more subtle ways, people who build Christian community can become emotionally and socially dependent on the group and the horizontal relationship can dominate the vertical.

I am arguing for the importance of both and that the vertical relationship between Christ and me does not become subverted. The people empowerment model functions on the premise that, as sisters and brothers in Christ, we mutually express our relationship with Christ in order to both give and receive. And so we are built up in the faith.

However, church is not the only place where our spirituality is formed and sustained. In our own personal lives, in the family and in the workplace there are opportunities for spiritual nourishment and growth and for service. There, too, we both give and receive. And there also Christ must be acknowledged as Lord.

Family fellowship and sharing with my wife, children and guests has played an important part in my own Christian formation. So have Bible studies and prayer meetings during several periods of secular employment. And the opportunity for fellowship, encouragement and nurture within the context of work in a Christian organisation working with troubled young people was frequently as meaningful as church.

Living with Christ and serving him wherever we are must remain the central reality of our lives. Church meetings cannot be our sole preoccupation even though they are very important.

Second, the lifestyle Jesus advocated must be central

The old idea that the Gospels are mainly biographical writings and the epistles are primarily theological treatises is no longer tenable. Since Rudolph Bultmann, scholars have rightly emphasised that the Gospels were written by members of the post-Easter community of faith with the needs of the church community in view. As such, the Gospels are primarily theological writings seeking to facilitate the life and ministry of the early churches by strongly focussing on the life and teachings of Jesus. In this, they are a balance to the writings of Paul.

I am not about to embark on a bit of "Paul bashing" in order to elevate Jesus. We have seen a lot of that in the name of New Testament scholarship: "Jesus was the radical, Paul the conservative"; "Jesus brought into being a social movement to liberate the marginalised and the poor, Paul created the middle-class urban house churches"; "Jesus brought freedom and dignity to women, Paul reasserted the old ideas of women's subordination."

The problem with these contrasting themes is that they are too simplistic and overdrawn. We have already seen that there are key liberative themes in Paul's writings, including his emphasis on freedom in Christ, the breakdown of racial, social and sexual divisions in Christ, and his emphasis on the church as people of God free from the old guardianship of Law and priest. We only need to remind ourselves again of the significance of Galatians 3, verse 28.

However, there is an important difference between the Pauline writings and the Gospels. The former see the life of faith, the nature of church and our service to the world flowing out of a faith relationship with the "cosmic" Christ. The latter emphasise the celebration of the messianic lifestyle based on the following of the historical Jesus.

Put differently and more simply, the epistles focus on the life of discipleship as a consequence of the risen Christ. The Gospels, on the other hand, focus on discipleship as a response to following the Jesus of "beard and sandal." In other words, Paul's emphasis is on mystical union by faith with the heavenly Christ who empowers us to live in the Spirit. The Gospels, on the other hand, call us to live life on the road with Jesus.[3]

There are several important implications that follow from this. The first (and not so germane to our overall argument) is that Paul's emphasis on "life in the Spirit" can leave the notion of discipleship rather vague. The Gospels' depiction of discipleship, however, tends to be more concrete. It has to do with an obedient following of Jesus, a life of renunciation, exercising a servant leadership, and living a life of joyful abandonment in the kingdom of God.

The second implication, however, is more specifically focussed and this is the main reason for developing this argument here: the Gospels' emphasis on life together is much less a church-focussed notion than the perspective we find in Paul's writings. In other words, the Gospels' notion of community is focussed on sharing in the mission of Jesus rather than emphasising elders and spiritual gifts for building up the body of Christ.

This Gospel viewpoint provides an invitation to us to take our search for a new way of being church a little more lightly. For while the Gospels see Jesus in solidarity with his disciples (Mark 3, verses 13 to 19 and Luke 8, verses 1 to 3), the focus is on being on the road with Jesus, and thereby responding to needs and challenges along the way. The emphasis in the Gospels is not simply on building community. It is on living life with Jesus. This life is kaleidoscopic in its diversity and possibilities. It leads us to prayer as well as to casting out demons. It draws us to the marginalised as well as to confront those who are in power. It calls us to a life of abandonment without withdrawal from life.

156

There is a dynamic in the Gospels that reminds us of the play *Godspell* where Jesus is displayed not as the ever- so-serious Son of God resplendent with ecclesiastical halo, but as the happy wonder-worker caught up in the joy of life while at the same time reaching out in compassion to those in need. Or, to change the image, in the carefree and happy abandonment of St. Francis of Assisi we sense a Christ-like approach to life.[4] This emphasis, which in its most concentrated form occurs in the Sermon of the Mount (Matthew 5 to 7), suggests a lifestyle that takes God seriously and ourselves lightly.

So much of Christianity has taken itself far too seriously and God not seriously enough. As a result, we have elevated our dogmatic formulations over that of Scripture. We have concretised our ecclesiastical structures. And our role in the world has been that of puritanical, and at times fanatical, moral guardians. We have constantly attempted to manage society in God's name. The church from Constantine through to the enlightenment of the eighteenth century sought to control society either by direct ecclesiastical power or by working in concert with the political forces of their day. The church consequently took itself very seriously. It was one of the significant power brokers in the machinations of those times.

The Gospels, on the other hand, call us to see God's kingdom power at work without negating our responsibility for action and service. And it challenges us to embrace an other-worldly wisdom where the poor are rich, the weak are strong and servants are powerful.

The idea of the upside-down kingdom where God's way is so vastly different than our normal way of doing things should suggest to us that being God's people by celebrating a messianic lifestyle should set us apart from normal institutional and organisational realities. In institutions and organisations, structures, management systems, roles, tasks and functions predominate. In the community of Jesus, friendships and ministry are primary. And the ministry focus involves including the marginalised in society.

Through this broad brushstroke, we can see that the Gospels balance out the Pauline emphasis, which runs the risk of an over-focus on Christian community life and the life of responsibility viewed in terms of certain priorities—such as the family and master-slave relationships. The Gospels dynamite structure and all narrowly-defined priorities. Instead, they emphasise lifestyle values that acknowledge God's concern for the world, particularly the small and the weak, and celebrate the power of doing God's will.

Here forgiveness, the embrace, the extra mile, the joy of reconciliation, the power of prayer, the way of abandonment, the strength of friendship, the reality of healing and the joy of liberation predominate. And though the Gospels give us principles for reconciliation (Matthew 18) and the broad sweep of life together (Mark 10, verses 29 to 31), we are hard-pressed to find structures for the shape of the community of Jesus.

It is interesting to note that the Gospels post-date the early Pauline writings (Romans, Galatians, 1 and 2 Corinthians) by several decades. They may therefore be called "revitalisation literature," since they strongly bring into view an anti-structural emphasis and the celebration of the messianic lifestyle that turns the world's values upside down. With this emphasis, the Gospels may well have served the early Christian communities with a powerful reminder that the primacy of life together is not certain structures, but the glad abandonment of following Jesus.

The Gospels suggest that if we take care of God's concerns then the other things will fall into place. We tend, however, to be too busy making sure that all the other things are in place first. These may include our security, position, well-being—and our churchly priorities. When these are all in place, we believe, we will be ready for God's concerns in the world. As a result of this approach, we construct our comfortable church buildings first and then think about how to serve our neighbourhood. We don't think about serving the general community first and making do with existing buildings and resources in the area. Thus we claim to build our churches for the glory of God, while we advertise that people can now worship in air-conditioned comfort.

Yet if we operate in this way, we might never get around to the matters of the kingdom. The matters of church are always so demanding and the special outreach to women in prostitution will just have to wait until we have our pre-school program for our church members established. Yet the matters of the kingdom require our attention now, as we go along—not when we have everything else ready. You can't wait until you are married. Or your children have grown up. Or you are financially secure. Or until you have set up all the appropriate structures. In the lifestyle of the kingdom, you need to seize the day.

I remember one coastal city church which took such a long time setting up a program for reaching young people on their way to north Queensland that, by the time everything was set up, itinerant youth had ceased to pass through the town! This illustration should not be seen as an argument against planning. But it is an argument for much greater flexibility and spontaneity.

The challenge of the messianic lifestyle is that it frees us from taking ourselves too seriously. It frees us from an over-preoccupation with our own structures for Christian community. At the same time, it frees us to express the truth that living life with Jesus, wherever we are in following him in the world, is essential to what it means to be the people of God.

I remember a friend of mine who brought a bunch of roses to a very irate newsreporter. This was a bigger factor in her conversion than all the "witnessing" she had been subjected to. A farmer friend of mine, who provided hospitality for our staff as well as for the drug addicts we were working with, once laughingly told me how he had been through many sessions at the local Pentecostal church to receive "spiritual renewal." But all to no avail. However, several weeks later, while rounding up some cattle and trying to hustle them towards home and thinking anything but godly thoughts, he found himself lying on his back loudly ecstatically praising God.

And more closely to the subject of this book, while reaching out to the young people on the streets of our city, particularly those in the drug scene, we made our base in an old Roman Catholic ex-convent. Some twenty of us lived together, shared our resources, worked together in this ministry, prayed and played together and shared the convent with young travellers, drug addicts and people in prostitution.

All of this was spontaneous and immediate. We had fun. We ministered. We worked hard. We spent a lot of time praying and often didn't know where our next meal would come from. But God changed lives even in the midst of our raucous early morning parties when, after having worked on the streets till 2.00 a.m., we were beyond tiredness and the need to go to bed.

Yet we had Christian community, even though we had not heard the term and read books about it. That all came later. And in the hindsight of nearly twenty-five years, I am not all that sure whether all the reading, the theologising, the historical reflection and the thinking about models and structures of Christian community made later forms of community that we experienced any better.

In those "innocent" days, focussed on loving and serving Jesus by also getting our hands dirty with the pain of the tragedies of broken lives, we had the reality of community as a gift which, in many ways, was better than our own subsequent endeavours to make community happen.

This lighter note is not an invitation to frivolity, but it mellows the emphasis on responsibility. While people empowerment has its basis in a life of responsibility, this can only be sustained when it is impregnated with hope and celebration. And if our life together is not so fragile that it doesn't require constant prayer for God's life and sustenance, then maybe we have taken too much on our own shoulders and have missed the ultimate blessing—which is that this kind of life is God's gracious gift.

Paul is not unmindful of this. For him, grace feeds responsibility, and freedom in Christ modifies our emphasis on structure. Thus, empowerment for responsibility, a key motif in understanding church, involves responsibility not only in being church, but also in serving the world. But this exercise of responsibility always flows out of the joyful following of Jesus, whose grace sustains us along the way.

ENDNOTES

1. Paul D. Hanson, *The People Called: The Growth of Community in the Bible*, Harper and Row, 1986.

2. Dietrich Bonhoeffer, *Life Together*, SCM, 1954

3. See Athol Gill, *Life on the Road*, Lancer, 1989.

4. See Johannes Jörgensen, *Saint Francis of Assisi: A Biography*, Doubleday, 1955.

CONCLUSION

This book promotes a new way of being church. It does so because the old way is fast becoming irrelevant through its failure to respond to the creative impulses of our time. I have identified these impulses under the theme of people empowerment.

In the face of the massive politicisation and technologisation of modern life, there are signs everywhere to be seen of people who are rightfully reclaiming more control over their own lives. I am advocating that these impulses should be creatively applied to the life and structures of the contemporary church. Rather than lamenting that the church is too modern and that its future lies in returning to older ways, I am asserting that the church is not modern enough. It is out of step with the contemporary emphases which claim that we learn by doing and we grow by assuming responsibility.

To illustrate this I have used the example, among others, of trends in community development where the emphasis is on working *with* people rather than *for* people, which has so frequently perpetuated dependence.

When I brought the issue of people empowerment to Scripture, I sought to show that there was a strong emphasis on people in solidarity or community growing together in Christ and assuming responsibility for their life together and their mission to the world. As sons and daughters of God, they were no longer to be under guardians. I thus sought to achieve a "fusion of horizons."[1]

This is the art of bringing contemporary questions to the Bible in such a way that these questions may invoke new insights from the Bible without imposing contemporary values on Scripture. In other words, the fusion of horizons operates on the premise that our horizon must not dominate the horizon of Scripture. In this process, we discovered that the Bible enhances our understanding about people empowerment and the growth of people for responsibility and mission.

This all led to the conclusion that the church is a significantly destructured and de-institutionalised reality where people come together in many different ways for the purpose of worship, teaching, sacrament, prayer, fellowship, encouragement, care and service.

The priority is not a particular model of being together— the hallmark is not that it is necessarily a house church, an intentional community or a deinstitutionalised traditional church structure. The hallmark of the church is rather that it is *people empowering*. And it seeks to achieve this characteristic by placing into the hands of the people the responsibility for determining their life together and their mission to the world under the Lordship of Christ and his word. I am not saying house churches or base ecclesial communities are the models to emulate. Nor am I denying their value. My focus has been very different. Instead of emphasising *models*, I have focussed on *processes*. My argument, then, has been that *any* model of church is commendable providing that it promotes people empowering processes.

This idea of church is very different from that which applies management procedures to the life of the church. It does so because the life together of Christians should not be further technologised. Instead, church is seen as the household of faith, not as an institution. Processes rather than structures should characterise the life of believers.

The preoccupation of much of the contemporary church in the West has been with numerical growth, right procedures, effective roles, departmentalisation, "top down" management and extensive programming. The result has largely been the movement of Christians from smaller churches to the larger ones which are able to provide a larger range of religious services. The approach taken in this book is to argue for a reversal in this trend and for the people themselves to take responsibility for their life together.

When we ask what these processes are that build such a life together, then we must speak of joining or community-building, mutual encouragement and care, learning by doing, challenge and common decision-making. As part of these processes, I envisage not only praying together, but also celebrating life together. I picture not only listening to Scripture together, but also serving the wider community together.

In other words, community-building has to do with holism. It has to do with being concerned about a brother's or sister's job as much as his or her spirituality. It includes Bible study, but also celebrating birthdays and other important events in people's lives. It may involve a night of poetry reading as much as a brief teaching module on contemporary theology. It involves baby-sitting and helping each other in many practical ways. In one case, it actually meant building an extension to someone's house. It may also mean helping someone shift house or to do some painting.

But Christian community is never simply for its own sake. It is building a life together in order to affect the world. Some have majored on taking troubled people into their homes and lives. Others have sponsored refugees and helped them to settle into their country. Others again have been involved in a range of neighbourhood projects. Most, however, have seen their daily work as the place for witness and ministry.

In achieving this new idea of church in some cases, the church will destructure itself to become this people empowerment model. In other cases, this way of being church will have to exist alongside the institutional church—as is the case with Catholic base ecclesial communities. Some may build this way of being church underneath the traditional model, while others may need to withdraw from the traditional church to create this type of fellowship.

This model of church is primarily a counter-community. Its motive is to live a different lifestyle, but nevertheless to be a witness in the world. It does not see its task as needing to build ecclesiastical structures that can compete with the power structures of the world and thereby exercise its influence in the world. Just as the Old Testament kingship and the church's attempt at rulership in the Middle Ages did not work, so the church's contemporary role is not to manage society.

Instead, the church is a "little flock" called to live its life in the midst of the world to the sound of a different drummer. Its call to proclaim good news, to work for social justice and to transform society will come from its obedient following of Christ and not from its attempt to play power politics. The impulse is to live with integrity in serving the world and this has little to do with using worldly methods. One need only think of the moral influence that a small community such as Sojourners in Washington, USA, can exercise.

At the beginning of this book, I said that I hoped it may be of some help to certain groups of people. It is appropriate to spell out now where I believe this help lies.

For those who have already left the church through frustration and alienation, there is a way to start again—providing this is done on the basis of forgiveness and exploration. Since forgiveness changes our reactive stance to a proactive one, and exploration gives us the time to work the old out of our system, there is the possibility to start anew.

In fact, you owe it to yourself and to your fellow believers to start again, because in one sense you have never "started" in the first place. Church is not meant to be under guardians. It is meant to be a place where you work out your responsibility in concert with others. Such a new way of being church is never easy to leave, because it is no longer a case of "them" (the clergy, the hierarchy, the decision-makers) and "us." It is a case of "us" and "us"—where we have a part to play with others in creating our life together.

I also had the immobilised in the church in view—those who are unhappy with their experience of church, but remain there. Over the years, I have met many who believe that church should be significantly different. Some wanted it to be more human. Others more relevant. Some wanted it to be less formal. Others more authentic. But they did nothing about it.

Frequently, in probing the reasons for their inaction, it became apparent to me that they had been mystified by the church's power and permanence. They had begun to believe that things could not be any different. They needed to be suspicious.

There is nothing permanent about the church. It is simply the solidification of the decisions of fragile men and women of the past. We need only think again of the beginnings of the Methodist or the Pentecostal churches. While the reasons for new beginnings have been subsequently clad in weighty historical explanations, they are finally no more weighty than the new beginnings you are challenged to make in concert with others. I trust that the shroud of mystification has been rent sufficiently for you to dare to catch the wind and harness it for your journey of faith.

One further group I addressed was young people. In my earlier comments, I was hard on them, caught up as they were in a "bless-me" Christianity that dares little and risks nothing. I don't blame them for their lack of radicalism. They are truly the products of their age. The 1980s, in particular, shaped the values where big is beautiful and greed is good. Both their world and their church have failed to teach them to seize the day and to make their unique contribution.

I can understand that young people prefer the safety of the traditional church structures and that they fail to be impressed with many of the more radical community experiments of the late 1960s and early 1970s, because they were small and tenuous and lacked the glossy edge that became so important in the 1980s. But many of the Christian young people of that time at least gave it a try. They took Jesus away from the stained glass window above the altar and put him in the street.

Sadly, the Jesus movement was shortlived and quickly commercialised—but it was an attempt. And many went the challenging road of attempting Christian community and forged new ministries of social concern and justice. There are those who are still joyfully walking this same road. Many house churches, Catholic covenant communities and intentional Christian communities are enjoying a twenty-year history.

The issue for you who are part of this present generation of young people is to catch a new vision that is sufficiently believable to warrant risks and hard work—a vision strong enough to take you out of the safety of the sanctuary onto the road with Jesus in a new form of glad abandonment.

I also have written for the clergy. They might feel particularly aggrieved—they might well feel that I have attacked them. In fact, that has been the furthest thing from my mind. I, also, am a clergyperson and I do not make light of the pressures that the clergy today are under.

Instead of attacking clergy, I have attacked the system. The clergy's role of virtually doing everything to keep the system going and trying to keep a group of people happy and blessed while giving them no real responsibility is a recipe for disaster. Not only has this led to many clergy leaving the ministry, but to serious emotional and physical breakdown on the part of some. It has also left their people dissatisfied and unhappy.

The call for a "people empowerment" model of church takes the pressure off clergy to "make it all happen" by placing the responsibility where it belongs—on the people of God themselves. This means that their role will have to change significantly, but their theological skills will still be required.

I can't see how denominational leaders can possibly be happy with these contours of the coming church. The church of the future is more a people movement than an institutionally driven entity. Church in this way is a grassroots and relational entity, no longer conceived in board rooms of the church's administrative centres. My hope, however, is that in time the people empowerment movement will become strong enough to win over these leaders.

And finally, what can I say to the theologians? It is simply this: your task has never been to defend the *status quo*, but to read Scripture afresh in the light of the new issues of our time. Many theologians are doing this by grappling with the pressing issues of world poverty and world debt and with the impending threat of ecological disaster. Alongside these and other important issues, I wish to place the matter of church family on the agenda once more.

This book is primarily an invitation to dialogue. It is not a blueprint of what the church should look like—no-one can predict this. But we do need theologians to work more closely with experiments to make church a more authentic place.

From the second and third centuries onward, the church became the place of the bishop, the priest and the altar.

In the Reformation era, the church became the place of the pulpit and the preacher.

In a new Reformation, may the church become a diverse movement of grassroots groups structured for empowerment, responsibility and mission and devoid of the institutional trappings that presently hamper its liberation.

ENDNOTES

1. See Hans-Georg Gadamer, *Truth and Method*, Seabury, 1975.

Appendix:

A Model for Change

This book has not focussed on bringing about structural changes in the contemporary church by spelling out specific contours. Instead, it has given priority to processes that are people-empowering. Consequently, I have spoken about catching the wind and changing tack. I have not sought to get down to specific details.

I have not taken this course because I do not have specific models in view. Instead, I believe in exploration. It's a time for further experimentation, not for closure. Moreover, different people in different situations will work these ideas out in very different ways. Hence, I have attempted to sketch the broad picture only.

However, I am acutely aware that there are readers who are looking for something more specific. I very hesitantly respond to their needs. I will, therefore, spell out a model which I think is readily achievable. *But I don't necessarily think it is the best.*

am not even sure if it is particularly good. But it may provide a practical starting point for further discussion and exploration.

AN ACHIEVABLE MODEL

This particular model operates on cell groups (or growth or care groups) meeting during the week and a combined meeting on Sundays. The mid-week cell group meets for fellowship, worship, prayer, sharing, Bible study, celebration of Holy Communion, fun nights, learning and doing combined ministry and outreach projects. The cell will usually consist of about ten adults plus children. In meeting together, they may share a meal and do some of the things elaborated above. There may also be special events for the children who are regarded as integral to the group.

The cell leadership operates on a rotating coordination basis for a period of two or three months. The group's internal program is decided by the group. The coordinator has the task to make sure that the agreed activities happen. Moreover, the group also decides the outreach ministry priorities in which it will engage.

Not only do most of the things that normally happen in church take place in the cell group, but the group functions to empower people. People learn the processes of community building. They learn how to facilitate a group. They learn how to do Bible study. And they learn how to be involved in various forms of ministry to the wider community. Hence, there is the need for special resource persons such as the theologically trained, but also those trained in the social sciences who have group building and group enabling skills.

The real life together takes place in the cell. But the cells are to be open, not exclusive. They will invite guests and particularly "seekers" who are those who are interested in the Christian life, but have made no firm commitment. Moreover, to overcome the possible problems of exclusivity, it is envisaged that within two years all members will rotate.

Where one has a plurality of such cells (and I am thinking of about seven to ten cells), then each week a particular cell has the overall coordinating responsibility for what takes place at the Sunday combined meeting.

While there may be a constancy of some elements such as worship, teaching, supper together either before or after the meeting and a special program for the children, the Sunday meeting will vary depending on the contribution that the members of the cell together with others will bring to the meeting. Issues that affect the cells as a whole or things that affect the Sunday combined meeting may arise from a particular cell for discussion by all the cells for a final decision. But the focus is to keep general issues down to a minimum.

What is potentially constructive about this model is that the reality of life together as the people of God happens in the cell. The purpose of the combined meeting is to promote the value of the input of others. Moreover, it fits with my major thesis—that people empowerment must be the key to what it means to be church, lest we fall back to models and structures that create dependence or the split-level church consisting of those who do the work and those who are largely spectators.

DISCUSSION QUESTIONS

PREFACE & INTRODUCTION

1. Which category of reader are you:
    a. One of the "stranded"—those who have worked tirelessly for change in the institutional church and have given up?
    b. One of the "valiant few"—those who have attempted alternative ways of being church?
    c. One of the "alienated"—those who have severed links with the church?
    d. One of the "unhappy"—those who are dissatisfied with the church, but remain immobilised?
    e. A young person who still has to experience the call of the radical Jesus or push for change?
    f. None of the above? (Come on, tell us.)

2. Do you believe that the church needs to change? If so, do you believe structures as well as individuals should change? Or are you basically happy with the way things are and feel this talk about "change in the church" is misplaced?

Try and describe *exactly* what you do feel about church and your part in it.

3. Describe how each of the following would be handled: first, from an institution-centred approach; second, from a people-centred approach:
   a. The encouragement of church members to exercise their gifts
   b. The handling of a dispute within the leadership of the church
   c. The planning of a worship program for a Sunday service.

4. Do you think that the introduction of the ordination of women has brought real change to the church's structures or not? Has it been a demonstration of the essence of the gospel, or a detraction from it? Explain your position.

5. How does history appear to support the idea that change is inevitable in "the church of the future" (see pages 19-20)? What is the criticism levelled in this Introduction at the *way* these changes have come? What is your view?

6. Do you agree with the author's assessment that "the church does not easily and readily embrace significant change" (page 18)? How is this different from change as a knee-jerk response to some crisis in the church—internal or external?

7. Which of the following do you see as the *essence* and which the *form* of church:
   a. the way Holy Communion or the Lord's Supper is conducted?
   b. the place of Jesus in the church?
   c. the emphasis on the liturgy or the preached word?
   d. the role of the clergy and other full-time professionals?

e. the fostering of a sense of community in the church? How did you decide which was which? Why is a distinction between form and essence important?

CHAPTER 1: A PERSONAL JOURNEY OF CHANGE

1. Tell/write down your own story about church. What has been your experience? Are you able to describe what you have learnt about (page 31):
   a. the importance of friendship?
   b. the church's mission to the world?
   c. openness to the wider traditions of the church?
   What would you add as key themes in *your* spiritual pilgrimage?

2. Summarise what can be learnt from the author's Aboriginal mission experience (pages 30-31). How accurate a picture is this of church generally, do you think? Does this resonate with any of your experiences?

3. Think about the relationship between friendship (or fellowship) and the formal structures of the church. Are these an either/or matter, or can we keep both in creative tension?

4. The concept of community has been critical to the author's understanding of church: "Community is being friends together in Christ in order that we can continue Christ's work in our world" (page 34). What, for you, is the core concept of church?

5. If you had been given a choice, what experiences of church would you like to have had? In particular, comment on the value to you of any of the following:

a. living in an intentional Christian community (i.e. where decisive action is taken to live together)
b. working in a Christian mission or parachurch organisation
c. being involved in helping to found exactly the church you wanted.

If you have experienced one of these, how has it shaped you? Were there any negative aspects?

CHAPTER 2: THE POLITICS OF CHANGE

1. "Change should be a matter of moving ourselves and others to live more authentically as God's people in our world" (page 39). What is meant by this statement? What questions, then, should we be asking when deciding whether some church practice should be changed or kept?

2. "[The church] is God's idea, but church is also a human institution." If this is true, what aspects are open to change, and what are not? Make as succinct a list as possible of the "unchangeables"—and then of the "changeables."

3. Why do human institutions like the church change so little? How does understanding why change is so slow help to bring it about?

4. How do you believe a "safe place" where concerns and new ideas can be explored (page 40) can be created? Why do many attempts to do this fail?

5. What criticism is levelled here at the "new" Christian movements of the 1960s and 1970s? What warning is there

here about what needs to be done if real change is to take place?

CHAPTER 3: AN APPEAL FOR CHANGE

1. In what practical ways can the church make the hopes, aspirations and struggles of its people central in:
   a. its teaching?
   b. its church programs?
   c. its liturgy?
   Why has this been so difficult to do?

2. How has the church's strong emphasis on *male* headship and leadership impacted on marriages? How does this reveal the way in which the church is dominated by "cognitive knowledge transfer" from the church to the people?

3. What objections does the author have to our choosing a church on the basis of whether the members have the same emphasis and interests as we do? What does the common concern for joining with those who are similar to us show about the way our churches operate?

4. How can each of the following areas of human experience be incorporated into our worship:
   a. the pressure a business person faces at work?
   b. the wonderful party some teenagers had the night before?
   c. the difficulties a migrant has in fitting into society?
   d. ways to spend quality time with our children?

5. Why is there often lack of recognition of the *informal* witness and service of members of churches? Why does the official

CATCH THE WIND

church program of witness and service receive priority over these? Should it?

CHAPTER 4: THE BARRIERS TO CHANGE

1. Think about Karl Rahner's distinction between an "open" and "boundary-centred" group (page 70). How can we make "outsiders" feel more at home? What other ways can we reduce the sense of "us" and "them"?

2. What are the practical outworkings that you have observed in people's everyday lives of the following:
   a. churches that are divided on socio-economic or racial grounds?
   b. male leadership of churches (see page 73)?
   Are there any redeeming features in these models?

3. Bearing in mind the lessons of history (pages 74–80), make a list of those elements you would have once thought were *essential* for a church to be a church, but that you now no longer believe to be so. In what ways have you changed *your* emphasis over the years?

4. What current practices of the church do you feel are likely to have no scriptural support? You may find it helpful to consider the following:
   a. the various forms of church worship services
   b. church buildings and property
   c. clergy-laity distinctions.
   Are there other reasons, apart from Scripture, *for* the above?

5. How could churches be restructured to provide "greater honour" to the weak, the poor and the marginalised (page 80)? Among other matters, you might look at areas like:

a. who leads our church services and how they are
   conducted
b. financial and administrative priorities for individuals and
   congregations
c. witness and service to the wider community.

6. Can any denomination truly claim to be "the New Testament church" (see pages 80–82)? Do you agree with the author's conclusion that the New Testament offers us a *range* of models rather than one ideal model? If so, what are the implications of this?

CHAPTER 5: THE IMPERATIVE FOR CHANGE

1. What would be an appropriate "mission statement" (i.e. a means of producing good outcomes) for your church? Bear in mind such specific elements as:
   a. helping people through their marriage problems
   b. supporting those with work or family problems
   c. holding in check dominant personalities
   d. teaching people the content of the Christian faith and how to live it in their everyday lives
   e. creating opportunities for corporate worship and praise, and developing people's trust in God.

2. How are the services provided by the church often institutionally- rather than people-driven? Explain in your own words how it works (see page 86).

3. Why is the church so often *not* in the forefront of desirable change? How has the mentality of the state church, *corpus Christianum* (page 91), held us back?

4. Are there strengths for the church when it starts from a position of weakness? How is this a useful antidote to the triumphalist, management-based, success-oriented view of the church?

5. What lessons in each of the following areas can the church learn from the "human service delivery" industry (page 93):
   a. the community identifies its own needs?
   b. people are mobilised to achieve their own outcomes?
   c. the patient is an active participant?
   d. the expert's controlling role is minimised?

   Is it legitimate for the church to learn from such "secular" areas? What is the difference between being "worldly" and being "relevant" (page 95)?

CHAPTER 6: THE SOURCE FOR CHANGE

1. What view of *Scripture* is the author setting up by his references to:
   a. the second and third century church?
   b. the Anabaptists?
   c. Martin Luther? (See pages 98–99.)
   What approach of the New Testament communities is the author seeking to recapture?

2. How does a "critical" reading of Scripture address the following issues:
   a. the three different models of New Testament churches (see page 100)?
   b. the diversity of teaching on the roles of women (see pages 103–104)?
   How comfortable do you feel with such thinking?

3. How does the church's treatment of the slavery issue support the present "rereading" of Scripture on the role and status of women? Does it worry you that much of the impetus for this change has come from outside the church? Do you think God sometimes uses "contemporary reality" for the good of the church?

4. What new insight has liberation theology brought to *our* understanding of the Bible? To what extent is it applicable to us, or is it a heresy to be rejected?

5. The author argues that contemporary thinking has forced Christians to ask new *questions*, but the *answers* still come from the Bible (page 106). What new questions are we being forced to ask for which, in many cases, we still have no clear answers from the Bible? You might consider, among other things:
   a. post-coital contraception (the "morning-after" pill)
   b. the apparent compromises required by democratically elected politicians to win office
   c. effective redistribution of the earth's resources.

CHAPTER 7: THE VISION FOR CHANGE

1. How does the "people empowerment" model differ from that of the 1960s "youth culture" model (see pages 110–111)? What does "freedom *for* responsibility" mean in practical terms?

2. How are the following passages of Scripture used to support the author's argument?
   Romans 12, verse 20 (page 112)
   Galatians 5, verse 1 (page 113)

1 Samuel 8, verses 11 to 18 (page 113)
Isaiah 42, verses 1 to 7 (page 115)
Galatians 4, verse 3 (page 116)
Colossians 2, verse 15 (page 116)

What point is being made that is a challenge to the traditional view of church? How did the pre-Vatican II Catholic and the Reformation churches adopt a model for church that worked *against* an understanding of "structural evil"?

How is this in contrast to the New Testament model? What is *one* helpful action that a church can take to empower individuals more?

4. If the Bible's emphasis is not on structures, what is it on? Select two passages that particularly bring this out (from pages 118 and 119, if you like)? Why do you think there is so little said about a structural model of church in the New Testament?

5. When we think of the church as a family rather than an institution, what does that mean for our view of:
   a. authority and leadership?
   b. gifts and talents?
   c. church organisation and programs?

How can we maintain the warmth and acceptance of each other that is characteristic of a good family and also the necessary "rules and regulations" of an orderly family?

CHAPTER 8: THE VISION IN ACTION

1. What are:
   a. intentional communities?
   b. base ecclesial communities?
   c. house churches? (See pages 128–131.)
   When are they most like the idea of church the author has?
   What do they need to guard against?

2. How does change come about in people, according to Peter Berger (page 134)? Why do you think such change is difficult? Think of any one situation at work, at home or in your own thinking where change has taken place for you in this way? If that has never happened, why do you think it hasn't?

3. Why does the author feel that the charismatic churches have moved back to the old pattern of church? What old pattern have they moved to (page 136)? Can you parallel this experience with any from your own life/that of your friends where substantial change has failed to take place for similar reasons?

4. Taking perhaps your own church (or, for that matter, any other institution), what is one practical step that could be taken to make decision-making more participatory? What would be the ramifications of such a step for:
   a. the position of those who have always had authority?
   b. the position of those who have not had it?
   c. the structures of the institutions?
   d. the potential for creativity?

5. Explain what the author means by:
   a. "This model favours *de*-institutionalisation, but it is not anarchic" (page 144)
   b. "This model maintains the importance of leadership" (page 145)
   c. "Elders do not need to have a positional role" (page 145)
   d. "People are basically not solo-gifted" (page 146).
   What are some difficulties associated with such thinking?
   Is it worth the challenge?

CHAPTER 9: A CHANGE OF LIFESTYLE

1. "Church is the matrix in which we are sustained, built up and empowered in order to be light, salt and leaven in the world" (page 153). What implications does this have for:
   a. what activities Christians should engage in when they are together?
   b. where the focus of their lives should be?

2. What does the author mean by saying that Christ, not the church, should be central (page 153)? Why does he see this as an important point to make? Do you feel that it is an important distinction, or merely the statement of the obvious?

3. Why is it necessary to place sufficient emphasis on adopting a Jesus lifestyle (page 155)? How can this help combat the twin problems of ecclesiastical power and social conservatism (see pages 156–157)?

4. "If we take care of God's concerns, then the other things will fall into place" (page 158). Create a scenario, real or imaginary, where churchly priorities could easily take precedence over God's concerns.

5. Think about the statement: "While people empowerment has its basis in a life of responsibility, this can only be sustained when it is impregnated with hope and celebration" (page 161).

   Think up some activities where we can celebrate together. Why are these an appropriate balance to our more serious activities as Christians? (Tie your answer in with Jesus' approach to life if you can.)

CONCLUSION

1. What is the critical test of whether a church is working as it should? Make an assessment of whether or not your church works according to this critical test. What would need to change for it to do so?

2. At what points have you found the book
   a. a challenge?
   b. a comfort?
   Share one of each together.

3. If you had to prepare a model for church, what would it be like? Is there value in having such a vision?

BIBLIOGRAPHY

D. Ashley and D.M. Orenstein, *Sociological Theory: Classical Statements*, Allyn and Bacon, 1985.

Willem Balke, *Calvin and the Anabaptist Radicals*, Eerdmans, 1981.

Robert Banks, *Paul's Idea of Community*, Anzea, 1979.

Robert Banks, *All the Business of Life*, Albatross, 1987.

Robert and Julia Banks, *The Church Comes Home: A New Base for Community and Mission*, Albatross, 1989.

Lois Barrett, *Building the House Church*, Herald, 1986.

Peter Berger, *The Social Reality of Religion*, Penguin, 1967.

Peter Berger and Thomas Luckmann, *The Social Construction of Reality*, Doubleday, 1966.

Richard J. Bernstein, *Beyond Objectivism and Relativism: Science, Hermeneutics and Praxis*, Basil Blackwell, 1983.

Donald G. Bloesch, *Wellsprings of Renewal: Promise in Christian Communal Life*, Eerdmans, 1974.

Conrad Boerma, *The Rich, the Poor and the Bible*, Westminster, 1978.

Clodovis Boff, *Theology and Praxis: Epistemological Foundations*, Orbis, 1987.

Leonardo Boff, *Church: Charism and Power*, SCM, 1985.

Dietrich Bonhoeffer, *Life Together*, SCM, 1954.

Emil Brunner, *The Misunderstanding of the Church*, Lutterworth, 1952.

David Clark, *Basic Communities: Towards an Alternative Society*, SPCK, 1977.

Stephen B. Clark, *Patterns of Christian Community: A Statement of Community Order*, Servant, 1984.

James Clinton, *Spiritual Gifts: A Self-Study and Group-Study Manual*, Horizon House, 1985.

J. Severino Croatto, *Exodus: A Hermeneutics of Freedom*, Orbis, 1981.

Avery Dulles, *Models of the Church*, Doubleday, 1974.

Donald Durnbaugh, *The Believer's Church*, Macmillan, 1968.

Vernard Eller, *The Outward Bound*, Eerdmans, 1980.

Jacques Ellul, *The Presence of the Kingdom*, Seabury, 1967.

Jacques Ellul, *The New Demons*, Seabury, 1975.

Jacques Ellul, *The Ethics of Freedoms*, Eerdmans, 1976.

Jacques Ellul, *The Subversion of Christianity*, Eerdmans, 1986.

Jacques Ellul, *The Technological Bluff*, Eerdmans, 1990.

Existence and Faith: Shorter Writings of Rudolf Bultmann, Schubert M. Ogden (ed.), Hodder & Stoughton, 1961.

Feminist Theology: A Reader, Ann Loades (ed.), SPCK, 1990.

Paul Feyerabend, *Against Method: Outline of an Anarchistic Theory of Knowledge*, NLB, 1975.

Elizabeth Schüssler Fiorenza, *In Memory of Her: A Feminist Theological Reconstruction of Christian Origins*, Crossroad, 1983.

M. & I. Fraser, *Wind and Fire*, Basic Communities Resource Centre, 1986.

Robert Friedmann, *The Theology of Anabaptism*, Herald, 1973.

Hans-Georg Gadamer, *Truth and Method*, Seabury, 1975.

Athol Gill, *Life on the Road*, Lancer, 1989.

Athol Gill, *The Fringes of Freedom*, Lancer, 1990.

Art Gish, *Living in Christian Community*, Albatross, 1980.

Gustavo Gutierrez, *The Power of the Poor in History*, SCM, 1983

Janet Hagberg, *Real Power: The Stages of Personal Power in Organisations*, Winston, 1984.

Paul D. Hanson, *The People Called: The Growth of Community in the Bible*, Harper and Row, 1986.

Michael Harper, *A New Way of Living*, Logos, 1973.

Peter Hodgson, *Revisioning the Church: Ecclesial Freedom in the New Paradigm*, Fortress, 1988.

Bengt Holmberg, *Paul and Power*, CWK Gleerup, 1978.

R. Hooykaas, *Religion and the Rise of Modern Science*, Eerdmans, 1972.

Anne Hope and Sally Timmel, *Training for Transformation: A Hand-book for Community Workers* (3 vols), Mambo, 1984.

Eric Jay, *The Church: Its Changing Image through Twenty Centuries* (2 vols), SPCK, 1977.

Luke T. Johnson, *Sharing Possessions: Mandate and Symbol of Faith*, Fortress, 1981.

Johannes Jörgensen, *Saint Francis of Assisi: A Biography*, Doubleday, 1955.

D. Keirsey and M. Bates, *Please Understand Me: Character and Temperament Types*, Prometheus Nemesis, 1984.

C. Norman Kraus, *The Authentic Witness*, Eerdmans, 1979.

Donald Kraybill, *The Upside Down Kingdom*, Herald, 1978.

Thomas S. Kuhn, *The Structure of Scientific Revolutions*, University of Chicago, 1962.

Steven Lukes, *Power: A Radical View*, Macmillan, 1974.

Thaddee Matura, *Gospel Radicalism: The Hard Sayings of Jesus*, Orbis, 1984.

Carlos Mesters, *Defenseless Flower: A New Reading of the Bible*, Claretian, 1990.

Jürgen Moltmann, *The Church in the Power of the Spirit*, SCM, 1977.

Jürgen Moltmann, *The Power of the Powerless*, SCM, 1983.

Helmut Richard Niebuhr, *The Social Sources of Denominationalism*, Scribner's, 1929.

Wilhelm Niesel, *Reformed Symbolics: A Comparison of Catholicism, Orthodoxy and Protestantism*, Oliver and Boyd, 1962.

David Nyberg, *Power over Power*, Cornell University, 1981.

James O'Halloran, *Signs of Hope: Developing Small Christian Communities*, Orbis, 1991.

Karl Rahner, *The Shape of the Church to Come*, SPCK, 1974.

Paul Riceour, *Hermeneutics and the Human Sciences*, CUP, 1981.

Lawrence Richards, *A New Face for the Church*, Zondervan, 1970.

Charles Ringma, *Seize the Day with Dietrich Bonhoeffer*, Albatross, 1991.

Charles Ringma, *Dare to Journey* with Henri Nouwen, Albatross, 1992.

Theodore Roszak, *The Making of a Counter Culture*, Doubleday, 1969.

R.J. Rushdoony, *The Institutes of Biblical Law*, Presbyterian and Reformed, 1973.

Trevor J. Saxby, *Pilgrims of a Common Life: Christian Community of Goods through the Centuries*, Herald, 1987.

Francis Schaeffer, *The Great Evangelical Disaster*, Crossway, 1984.

E.F. Schumacher, *Small is Beautiful: Economics as if People Mattered*, Harper and Row, 1973.

Juan Luis Segundo, *The Liberation of Theology*, Gill and Macmillan, 1977.

Ira Shor and Paulo Freire, *A Pedagogy for Liberation*, Bergin & Garvey, 1987.

Christian Smith, *Going to the Root: Nine Proposals for Radical Church Renewal*, Herald, 1992.

Howard A. Snyder, *Liberating the Church*, IVP, 1983.

Howard A. Snyder, *Signs of the Spirit: How God Reshapes the Church*, Academie, 1989.

Jon Soberino, *The True Church and the Poor*, Orbis, 1984.

F. Ernest Stoeffler, *Continental Pietism and Early American Christianity*, Eerdmans, 1976.

Studies in Empowerment: Steps Towards Understanding and Action, J. Rappaport, C. Swift and R. Hess (eds), Hawarth, 1984.

Willard M. Swartley, *Slavery, Sabbath, War and Women: Case Issues in Biblical Interpretation*, Herald, 1983.

Terrence Tilley, *Story Theology*, Michael Glazier, 1985.

The Challenge of Basic Christian Communities, S. Torres and J. Eagleson (eds), Orbis, 1981.

Jean Vanier, *Community and Growth*, Saint Paul, 1983.

Leonard Verduin, *The Reformers and their Step-Children*, Eerdmans, 1964.

Max Weber: *On Charisma and Institution Building*, S.N. Eisenstadt (ed.), University of Chicago, 1968.

Max Weber, *The Sociology of Religion*, Methuen, 1966.

Walter Wink, *Unmasking the Powers: The Invisible Forces that Determine Existence*, Fortress, 1986.

Benjamin Zablocki, *The Joyful Community*, Penguin, 1971.

INDEX

everyday life issues 51, 88

F

Fiorenza, Elizabeth Schüssler 93
Foster, Richard 62
Freire, Paulo 54, 110
Friedmann, Robert 75
friendship 34

G

Gadamer 110
Gadamer, Hans-Georg 52
Gandhi 109
gifts 145–146
Gill, Athol 55, 81, 136
Gospels 8, 81, 155–161
Green, Thomas 62
guardianship 115–117, 115–121,
146, 167
Gutierrez, Gustavo 85

H

Harper, Michael 137
Holmberg, Bengt 78
hospitality 8
house churches 11, 32, 33, 38, 46,
71, 78, 101, 128–130
House of Freedom 12, 129
House of the Gentle Bunyip 12,
129
House of the New World 12

I

intentional communities 11,
128–132

J

Jehovah's Witnesses 18
Jesus Christ

and leadership 57
and lifestyle 151–161
and Paul 155–159
Jones, Jim 61
Jubilee Fellowship 13, 34

K

King, Dr Martin Luther 109
Koinonia Farm 32
Koresh, David 61, 154
Kraybill, Donald 91
Kuhn, Thomas 109

L

L'Abri 32
laity 41–43, 51
Leadership 72–73
leadership 33, 41–45, 57–58, 60,
71, 78, 123, 141, 145–146
and the Bible 112–123
liberation theology 105–106
lifestyle of Christians 151–161
Luckmann, Thomas 78
Luther, Martin 98, 98–99, 103, 119
Lutheran church 17, 81, 140

M

Mary Sisters 32
May, Rollo 110
Merton, Thomas 62
Methodist church 167
middle-class 22
Moltmann, Jürgen 10
Moravians 31
Myers-Briggs assessment 146

N

Niebuhr, Helmut R. 50
Niesel, Wilhelm 75
Nouwen, Henri 31, 62

Printed in the United States
30162LVS00002B/268-285

9 781573 832663